FOCUSED

5 TIPS FOR PARENTS

- **Learn as much as you can about ADHD.** Choose books and other resources that provide practical strategies and real-world advice that you can implement right away or store for later use. Also, reach out to others who have raised kids with ADHD; they can be a great source of useful advice and information.

- **Be assured that ADHD can lead to success.** The more you know about how to manage ADHD in your child, the more confident you will be that you can make a difference. Many people with ADHD achieve great success. With the proper strategies and continued support, your child can thrive in school, at home, and in life.

- **Find the right fit for your child.** Many professionals with various specialties can help your child, but you don't need to hire every expert out there. Instead, explore your options and try to connect your child to specific activities and professionals that are best suited to their unique needs and interests.

- **Realize that change is a process.** The sooner you set a foundation for support, the sooner your child will benefit. However, you may not see obvious changes for some time. Have patience and know that with the right guidance and therapies, your child will learn, mature, and flourish—at your child's natural pace.

- **Remember, there's no one to blame!** Poor parenting does not cause ADHD, so if you've been playing the blame game, now is the time to stop and start turning your attention to what you can do to support your child—and yourself—from here on out.

FOCUSED

ADHD & ADD
Parenting Strategies
for Children with Attention Deficit Disorder

BLYTHE GROSSBERG, PSY.D
Author of *Making ADD Work*

ALTHEA
PRESS

For general information on our other products and services or to obtain technical support, please
contact our Customer Care Department within the United States at (866) 744-2665, or outside the
United States at (510) 253-0500.

Althea Press publishes its books in a variety of electronic and print formats. Some content that
appears in print may not be available in electronic books, and vice versa.

Cover photograph © fStop/Offset

ISBN: Print 978-1-62315-619-0 | eBook 978-1-62315-620-6

CONTENTS

A LETTER TO PARENTS

Children with ADHD are some of the most creative, dynamic, and enjoyable people I know. After being surrounded in college by people obsessed with "doing the right thing" to get ahead, I found working with kids with ADHD refreshing. Instead of relying on old standards, they are constantly inventing new ways of doing things.

As a learning specialist with more than fifteen years of experience working with children with ADHD and learning differences, I know that parents often struggle to find the right kinds of help for their kids. They may worry that their children will struggle more than their peers to lead happy and productive lives. However, the kids I've worked with have gone on to use their considerable strengths to develop strategies that work around their obstacles. With the right support, children with ADHD can be very successful—your child included.

Take Zach. When he was in eighth grade, his teachers wrote him off as hopeless. He was disruptive and unable to concentrate in class. As a result, his grades were so low that he was in danger of being held back. After Zach was diagnosed with ADHD, his parents consulted an experienced psychiatrist, who recommended medication that helped Zach concentrate. I also worked with Zach to help him develop strategies to organize his time and assignments and study effectively for tests. In the span of a year, to my delight, he became a solid "B" student, and he had time to devote to his true love—acting and writing plays. He thrived in high school and college as an accomplished actor and eventually went on to work as a screenwriter. Success stories like Zach's—and many other children I've worked with—fill me with hope for the future.

Your child can also find a happy and productive path like the one Zach found. This book offers you tried-and-true strategies to help your child reach their potential. You will learn ways to help your child transition more easily from activity to activity, meet behavioral expectations, channel their energy, and follow directions. In helping your child, you will also learn ways to channel your own energy into creating a more peaceful and manageable home. You will discover ways to work with your child's strengths and positive qualities to create a safe, supportive, and empowering home and school environment. If you also have ADHD, this book offers you a way to help yourself, too, so that the whole family flourishes.

ADHD-focused professionals in many fields are continuing to develop a better understanding of how to help those with ADHD. New strategies, therapies, pharmacological interventions, medications, and other medical advances are creating more options than ever before to help you and your child manage ADHD. *Focused* introduces you to this essential information.

In part 1, you will learn about the symptoms and nature of the ADHD diagnosis as well as common behavioral patterns associated with ADHD. Then, in part 2, you can turn straight to the material that can help the most—right now. The chapters are arranged according to age, from preschool to adult, with each chapter offering various approaches as well as parenting strategies to help you adapt and learn new ways to help your child thrive.

Blythe Grossberg, Psy.D
BROOKLYN, NY

PART ONE

The ADHD Diagnosis

When you first hear your child has ADHD, you will want to know how the diagnosis applies to them on an individual level. The first part of this book will familiarize you with symptoms that are common among some (but not all) children and adults with ADHD. You will also learn ways that people with ADHD handle their obstacles and use their strengths to achieve success.

CHAPTER 1

The Truth About ADHD

Let's get right to the basics: Attention deficit/hyperactivity disorder (ADHD) is a relatively common disorder of childhood, which has symptoms of inattention, hyperactivity, and impulsivity to differing degrees in different people. George Frederic Still, the so-called "father of British pediatrics," is widely credited with the first scientific description of what would eventually become known as ADHD in a series of lectures he gave in 1902, in which he described children who struggled with attention and self-regulation.

ADHD went by many names, until in 1968, when it became part of the *DSM-2* (the *Diagnostic and Statistical Manual of Mental Disorders*, published by the American Psychiatric Association), which physicians and other professionals use in diagnosing patients. At the time, the disorder was known as the hyperkinetic reaction of childhood. When the *DSM-3* was released in 1980, the condition was termed attention deficit disorder (ADD). This was later changed to attention deficit/hyperactivity disorder (ADHD) 1987, which is the term that has remained in use since. In 1994, the *DSM-4* presented subtypes of ADHD for a more complete description of the condition.

The general public has developed an increased awareness of ADHD over the past few decades. The positive result of this awareness is that many people with ADHD have been diagnosed properly, and are getting the help they need. The negative result is that many people who are not qualified to diagnose ADHD nonetheless diagnose the condition in children and others, leading to misinformation. Only a doctor, psychologist, or related health-care professional can diagnose ADHD.

According to the National Institute of Mental Health (NIMH), ADHD currently affects about 9 percent of children ages 13–18. (Statistics are not kept on younger children.) About 50 to 60 percent of children with this condition will continue to show symptoms into adulthood. While it is relatively common, ADHD is often misunderstood and cloaked in myth. This chapter will help you understand the diagnosis and symptoms of ADHD, so that you can begin separating myth from fact.

ADHD involves three core symptoms, or subtypes: inattentive, impulsive, and hyperactive. These are referred to as "presentations" in the *DSM-5*.

Symptoms in a Nutshell

Let's look at each of these core symptoms and their associated behaviors in this section. For a diagnosis of ADHD, the symptoms must be present before the child is twelve years old and must show up in at least two settings, such as school and home. The symptoms can also continue to be present in adults. Keep in mind that ADHD requires a professional diagnosis, so this information is provided just to give you some insight into your child's diagnosis.

Inattention

Children with ADHD can struggle to maintain their attention on longer, boring, or tedious tasks, or tasks that require multiple steps. They are often daydreamers who may tune out their teachers and parents, or seem restless and forgetful. They often don't keep track of their belongings or stay on task, and they may find it difficult to sustain attention for long periods of time or periods of time that are manageable to their peers. They may need greater stimulation or novel activities to be able to attend to tasks.

Impulsivity

Children with ADHD may struggle to control their impulses and regulate themselves. They may have little patience for waiting in line, following directions or rules, or listening to what other people say. They may speak out of turn or say whatever is on their mind, without filtering what they say. They often turn to stimulating or novel tasks rather than finishing less rewarding or less interesting tasks, and they may also often engage in risk-taking behaviors and have trouble managing money or time.

Hyperactivity

Some children with ADHD may be hyperactive, presenting with such symptoms as rapid speech or high activity levels. They may rush from activity to activity and may require constant stimulation to prevent boredom. They may show restlessness or increased activity and may often be out of their seat in school. They often come across as rude, loud, or uncontrolled.

These behaviors are often a normal part of development for many children under the age of seven. To warrant further investigation, children need to present these symptoms chronically, and they need to show these symptoms in all areas of life, including at school, at home, and during other activities. In addition, these symptoms cannot be explained by other factors, such as illness, stresses, or psychological conditions.

If you are reading this book because you suspect your child has ADHD, seek the help of a qualified professional—a pediatrician, family doctor, psychologist, psychiatrist, or other health-care professional. A family doctor can potentially diagnose ADHD based on the symptoms your child presents, while a psychologist or neuropsychologist might conduct a more comprehensive assessment that looks at your child's different cognitive functions. These types of psychoeducational assessments can be expensive and are often not covered by insurance (but be sure to check with your insurance company). Nevertheless, the best place to start is often with your family doctor, who can refer you to another professional if needed.

Common ADHD Myths

There are many common misconceptions surrounding ADHD—many of which you may have heard from well-meaning friends, family members, and maybe even some professionals. Let's look at each in turn, along with the reality that debunks each myth.

- **Myth #1: ADHD is itself a myth.** ADHD is a real disorder with identifiable symptoms that present themselves in similar ways in different children and adults. Recent studies have revealed differences between the brains of children with ADHD compared to their typically developing peers, particularly in areas of the brain related to attention, judgment, and planning. In addition, ADHD is often thought only to be a problem in the United States, but it is also present in other countries where it may be underdiagnosed due to a lack of awareness on the part of doctors. For example, according to Marilyn Wedge, PhD in her 2012 *Psychology Today* article, "Why French Kids Don't Have ADHD," about 0.5 percent of children in France have been diagnosed with ADHD and are being treated with medication, compared to 9 percent in the United States. As parents of children with ADHD know firsthand, the symptoms are not a creation of the pharmaceutical industry, medical establishment, or media.

- **Myth #2: ADHD is caused by the environment or food.** While this is an attractive idea, since it suggests that children and adults with ADHD can be cured by changing their environment or diet, evidence points to a genetic cause of ADHD and to issues related to brain development, rather than to the excess consumption of sugar, food additives, or environmental toxins. However, there's no doubt that proper nutrition does play a part in managing ADHD. (Diet is discussed briefly in chapter 4.)

- **Myth #3: ADHD is caused by poor parenting.** Parenting style cannot affect a child's genetic makeup, so with the genetic factor in mind, it is just not possible that ADHD can be caused by poor parenting. However, parents can play a large role in helping their child with ADHD learn coping skills and strategies to thrive in school and at home.

- **Myth #4: People with ADHD are less intelligent than their peers.** ADHD is a physiological condition that causes difficulty with attention, impulsivity, and hyperactivity. Unfortunately, because of these symptoms, children and adults alike fail to reach their potential in school or other settings until they find strategies that work well with their particular personality and cognitive style. In other words, ADHD can prevent children and adults with average or higher-than-average intelligence from reaching success until they learn to manage their symptoms, but ADHD is not a deficit in intelligence.

- **Myth #5: ADHD can be cured by taking a pill.** While several pharmaceutical treatments can help children and adults with ADHD manage their symptoms, medicine is not a cure-all. Pharmaceutical treatment, if recommended for a child, can help the child attend to and practice strategies to learn, manage impulsivity, follow directions, listen to others, stay organized, and carry out other tasks required in school and at home. While medicine can improve symptoms, it does not cure the disorder.

- **Myth #6: ADHD is overdiagnosed.** While the media commonly reports that ADHD medication is overprescribed, research organizations such as the NIMH believe that a more serious concern is that ADHD is often underdiagnosed or misdiagnosed as disorders with similar symptoms (such as childhood anxiety or depression). Medical and psychological professionals continue to refine the way they diagnose ADHD and differentiate it from other disorders.

  Russell Barkley, PhD, an internationally recognized authority on attention deficit hyperactivity disorder and the author of *Taking Charge of ADHD: The Complete, Authoritative Guide for Parents*, believes that about 80 percent of children with ADHD are now diagnosed, compared to the 1960s and 1970s when only about 20 percent of children who had ADHD were properly diagnosed. In other words, children with ADHD are more likely to be correctly diagnosed than in decades past, giving the impression that more children have the disorder than ever, which is not true considering about 20 percent of children with ADHD remain undiagnosed. In addition, while the numbers of adults diagnosed with ADHD has doubled in recent years, Barkley believes that the majority of adults with this condition are still untreated.

- **Myth #7: ADHD disappears as children mature.** While some children may outgrow some of the core symptoms of ADHD, such as hyperactivity, they may also continue to show some of the symptoms as they grow into adolescence and young adulthood. Commonly, hyperactivity declines, but inattention may continue to affect young adults, particularly as they are faced with the increasing complexity and independence of having a job and attending college. Some young adults continue to meet the full criteria for ADHD; others might not, but they may still present with some of the symptoms and behavioral problems of ADHD. When adolescence hits, sometimes other conditions emerge that often occur alongside ADHD, including depression, anxiety, bipolar disorder, and body image issues. It is important to continuously monitor your child's progression and evaluate—and reevaluate—to make sure your child is being treated properly and diagnosed correctly. (This is discussed further in chapters 7 and 8.)

- **Myth #8: Overly active children have ADHD.** While hyperactivity is one of the core symptoms of ADHD, not all overly active children will meet criteria for ADHD. Sometimes, high-achieving children are overly active in school because they are not being challenged—in other words, they are given developmentally inappropriate activities that require them to be sedentary, in mind or body, at a degree that does not align with their development or personality. A high activity level does not, in and of itself, mean that a child has ADHD.

THE ADHD ADVANTAGE

Sir Richard Branson, who founded Virgin (a group of over 400 companies, including Virgin Records and Virgin Atlantic Airways), is a multibillionaire and adventurer who is open about having ADHD, and known for his forward-thinking ways. He's attempted to circumnavigate the globe in a hot air balloon, and is currently developing Virgin Galactic, which may become the world's first commercial spaceline. Many experts believe that having ADHD enables entrepreneurs, such as Branson, to be more successful, because it gives them the drive to take risks and see possibilities that other people might not notice.

- Myth #9: Only boys have ADHD. Girls are underdiagnosed for ADHD. Typically, boys with ADHD display hyperactivity or impulsivity, particularly when they are young, so they may be easier to pick out of a classroom. Girls may also have hyperactive tendencies, but, according to experts such as Patricia Quinn, MD, Director of the National Center for Gender Issues and ADHD in Washington, DC, they tend to exhibit inattention, which makes the disorder harder to diagnose. Also, girls with ADHD generally tend to follow teachers' directions and to be more cooperative with parents. (One of the strategies offered in chapter 6 focuses specifically on girls with ADHD.)

- Myth #10: ADHD means failure. This myth has been proven untrue time and time again. Many top achievers use the unique abilities that well-managed ADHD can grant, such as the ability to multitask and follow through on great innovations. High-profile achievers such as Olympic gold medalist Michael Phelps have been upfront in the media about having ADHD. Clearly, ADHD can confer creativity and drive in people who have it, and many people with ADHD are very successful in fields that cater to their high energy and out-of-the-box thinking.

Causes of ADHD

As you have just learned (but probably already knew), ADHD is not caused by poor parenting—nor is this disorder caused by a school system focused on rote learning and sedentary behavior or by watching too much television or playing too many video games. A national study of teachers, kindergarteners, and first-graders showed that kindergarteners' time spent watching television was not associated with reduced attention in first grade. That's good to know, of course, but be aware that extended or frequent sedentary activities can exacerbate the core symptoms of ADHD. (Later, you will learn more about channeling your child's energy as well as other strategies so that sedentary activities become more doable.)

Let's now look at the current understanding of how ADHD does develop. Although research is ongoing, many neurological and medical professionals believe that ADHD is caused by genetic factors. For example, research on twins and their families has revealed that when one member of a family has ADHD, there is a much greater likelihood of other blood-related family members also having the disorder.

Other studies have shown that people with ADHD share certain commonalities in how their brains develop and function. Research conducted by the NIMH suggests that the brain's prefrontal cortex (which is involved with planning, organization, and self-control) may develop more slowly in people with ADHD. Other studies have suggested that people with ADHD may have irregularities in the way certain neurotransmitters, such as dopamine, function. Their impaired systems could explain why stimulant medications (such as amphetamines and methylphenidate) are effective in reducing symptoms of ADHD, as these medications increase the activity of dopamine in the brain. Also, according to some research, exposure to large amounts of alcohol or drugs (including the chemicals in cigarettes) in utero can increase the risk of a child's developing ADHD. Low birth weight has also been implicated in an elevated risk of the disorder.

Because the causes of ADHD are presently thought to be genetic and physiological in nature, children with ADHD cannot be blamed for their symptoms. The best approach is developing proper strategies to manage the symptoms and working at the child's own pace toward developing the maturity and the independence that may come more easily to those without ADHD. Regardless of the cause, you have a very valuable role in helping your child develop strategies and find treatments to manage the symptoms of ADHD and reach their potential.

Parenting a Child with ADHD

Although there are many theories and supporting research, the cause of ADHD is currently outside of the realm of certainty, even for medical professionals. Therefore, rather than trying to pinpoint how your child developed ADHD, and maybe even blaming yourself, your energy can be better spent helping your child learn ways to handle their symptoms as well as building some parenting skills that can help your child succeed—and reduce the tension in your home.

After an ADHD diagnosis, parents often worry that their child won't go on to lead a fulfilling life. However, as mentioned earlier, children with ADHD can lead happy, productive lives. Children with ADHD are often creative, dynamic, and gifted in areas such as invention, art, and social relations. In today's fast-paced, constantly changing world, ADHD can, in some ways, provide an advantage, as some people with ADHD thrive when they are able to adapt continuously and in conditions of uncertainty. Many children with ADHD find that mainstream schools do not reward their behaviors and interests, but they experience success in the adult world when they find a niche that caters to the way their mind works.

In recent years, the understanding of ADHD has matured to the point where parents are able to develop deeper insight into how ADHD specifically affects their child, giving them more opportunities to guide their child toward success in life. In addition, parents and professionals are also beginning to understand, not only the challenges of ADHD, but also the very real strengths of children with this condition. The next chapter discusses both.

COMMON COEXISTING CONDITIONS WITH ADHD

About two-thirds of children with ADHD have a coexisting condition, which may or may not be the case with your child. Speak with your child's doctor or other treatment professionals to explore all the possibilities. The following are some common conditions that often coexist with ADHD:

Learning Disorders: While ADHD is not a learning disorder, it commonly occurs with learning disabilities. Scientists are still trying to discover why many children with ADHD also have dyslexia or below-average math abilities. Some experts believe that the same genes that determine ADHD may also be related to the development of learning disorders.

Some children with ADHD have inattentive symptoms that complicate their ability to learn, and they may require specialized schools or settings to reach their full academic potential. A child with ADHD may require accommodations or changes in their school plan, such as seatings near the teachers, extra time on tests, or the ability to take breaks to reach their potential.

Mood Disorders: ADHD often coexists with mood disorders, such as anxiety and depression. In addition, ADHD may actually cause depression and anxiety, resulting from difficulty managing social situations and work-related tasks. If a child has both a mood disorder and ADHD, they may need therapies and/or medications that treat both of these conditions without worsening the symptoms of either one. In these cases, it is imperative to work with an experienced medical or psychological team.

Oppositional Defiant Disorder and Conduct Disorder: Many children with ADHD also struggle with oppositional and defiant behavior, such as not following directions; fighting with parents, teachers, siblings, and peers; and being verbally and physically aggressive. Additional therapies and treatments may be necessary to manage these symptoms.

Obsessive-Compulsive Disorder (OCD): This disorder is characterized by unwanted, recurring thoughts (obsessions) and repeated behaviors (compulsions), which may make it difficult for kids to stay on task. They may appear distracted and fidgety. These behaviors are often confused with ADHD and misdiagnosed. While OCD and ADHD can indeed exist together, it is critical to get a thorough and correct diagnosis. Stimulant medications can worsen OCD, so treating children who have coexisting ADHD and OCD requires the help of an experienced medical or psychological team.

Tic Disorders/Tourette Syndrome: Tic disorders, which involve sudden involuntary movements such as eye blinking or coughing, and Tourette syndrome, a genetic disorder that involves motor and vocal tics, often coexist with ADHD. Behavioral modification and certain types of medicine can be helpful in treating both conditions when they coexist.

CHAPTER 2

The Challenges of Growing Up with ADHD

Like all kids, children with ADHD can be charming, playful, and inventive. In fact, children with ADHD are often more inventive and high-spirited than their peers, and they are often more dynamic and creative. As a result, they have a wealth of ideas and projects they are working on, and if their parents and teachers recognize their talents and inspired natures, they can be quite engaging and fun to be around. Chances are you've experienced this aspect of your child's nature and can fully appreciate the times when things just seem to flow.

However, childhood can be difficult for everyone at times—and yes, it can be doubly hard for children with ADHD. These children may find themselves unable to keep up with their peers or, conversely, excelling past them in certain areas while falling behind in others. Scientific evidence points to the fact that children with ADHD mature more slowly than their peers do, but this does not mean they won't eventually catch up. It also does not mean they are oblivious to the differences that separate them from their peers, who they may see more often rewarded and applauded for socially acceptable behavior at home and school. Children with ADHD may seem "out of it" at times; while they may seem blasé about their performance or actions, they often acutely feel their assumed failures and earnestly want to do better. Yet they often have cognitive obstacles that make it difficult for them to actually behave better in school and at home without interventions and strategies tailored to the way their mind works. As a result, without the right help, they may suffer from a lack of self-confidence and develop an overly negative perspective.

While each child's path is different, many children with ADHD do not find their talents rewarded in traditional schools or at home. They may struggle to do what their parents, relatives, and teachers expect of them—keeping track of their belongings, finishing their homework, staying quiet while others are speaking, being tactful, and staying on task while completing chores. Their rooms may be messy, and their backpacks may look like the aftermath of an explosion. They may seem willfully disobedient, but many of them crave adult approval.

Many children with ADHD have the sensation of knowing that they could be perceived as talented—if their parents and teachers would take a minute to recognize their clever conversation, the poem they wrote, or the skyscraper they designed. So, keep in mind that although your child's room may look like a disaster area, under that mess may be a very clever model plane, or a pile of sketches, or a guitar and a pile of song lyrics they composed. Of course, these are just examples, but consider the possibility that, when it comes to your child, there are surprising discoveries to be made.

While it is true that children with ADHD may have very real talents waiting to be noticed, they also struggle with common challenges that usually do not escape attention, such as the following:

Common Challenges of Children with ADHD

- **Problems following directions:** Often, children with ADHD do not follow directions. Sometimes impulsivity or inattention makes it hard for them to follow oral directions, and they often do not read written directions carefully. They may seem like they are daydreaming instead of listening and seem willfully defiant, while they may actually want to obey.

- **Problems keeping track of belongings:** Children with ADHD struggle at ages far past those of their peers to keep track of their possessions. Parents of these children may tire of buying them replacement mittens, backpacks, notebooks, and phones.

- **Problems keeping track of time:** ADHD often causes children to have a poor sense of time. While other children seem to naturally internalize how long it will take them to do a task and how to arrive on time, children with ADHD can be very inefficient and lack a realistic sense of time. As a result, they can either rush through tasks with carelessness or devote far too much time to a task, working with great inefficiency.

- **Difficulty getting started on tasks:** For many children with ADHD, initiating tasks is one of the most difficult and challenging obstacles to overcome. They may procrastinate so long that they do not get started at all on tasks or need to rush heedlessly through them. Perfectionism can often go along with their difficulty with initiation; in other words, these children do not start tasks or work far enough in advance to get a good grade, but also have an unrealistic and pressing need to do these tasks perfectly, perhaps to quiet their own internal critic and the critics they often find surrounding them.

- **Difficulty completing tasks:** ADHD can cause children to go astray in the process of finishing tasks with multiple steps. They can struggle in each phase of a long task; starting the task, staying focused, following each mini-step involved in the task, completing the task, and shifting their attention to the next step.

- **A need for stimulation and activity:** While an appreciation for activity can help children become adventurers and athletes, it can also make them restless in school, houses of worship, or other formal settings. In addition, their need for constant stimulation can lead them to sometimes engage in thoughtless or rude behavior.

- **Frustration:** ADHD can cause children to get frustrated, as they can make errors and often feel that they are not living up to their potential. If these children also have difficulty controlling their moods and anger, it can make it hard for them to process feelings of frustration. They may, at times, lash out at those around them.

- **Low self-confidence:** While some children with ADHD may come across as having an unrealistically high level of self-confidence (as they don't always have a good sense of what they can reasonably accomplish), they may actually suffer from feelings of inferiority and a lack of self-worth for not being able to keep up with activities that may be easier for their peers to accomplish. They seem to intuitively know that they are different (even if they don't know they have ADHD), and they often have a sense of not measuring up, even if their parents and teachers praise them.

- **Social problems:** Some children with ADHD struggle to maintain socially acceptable behavior because their impulsivity may cause an inability to filter their words and consider their actions. As a result, they may find themselves unaccepted by their peers.

- **Academic problems:** Inattention and hyperactivity may result in behavioral or academic problems at school. These failures may be especially acute in a traditional school setting that values sitting still and carrying out rote written work over the expression of the individual. Children with ADHD tend to get bored in these settings and act out to relieve their boredom.

- **Problems with mood:** Children with ADHD often have to manage separate coexisting mood disorders, such as anxiety, depression, and bipolar disorder. (See Common Coexisting Conditions with ADHD on page 22.)

- **Trouble with sleep–wake cycle:** ADHD may cause children to have problems sleeping at night and staying awake during the day, so they may often look and feel sleepy in school.

Common Patterns of Behavior

Children with ADHD often have common patterns of behavior, depending on their ADHD subtype (see chapter 1). Being aware of your child's particular patterns can shed light on how your child can best be supported. Although these behavior patterns are common among kids with ADHD, they may manifest in different ways from child to child.

Inattention

Children with the inattentive subtype may be harder to recognize and diagnose at first, because they do not have the stereotypical restlessness and hyperactivity that many parents and teachers associate with ADHD. While they may not speak out in class, fidget, or interrupt others, children with the inattentive form of ADHD may truly struggle to simply be present. They are often lost in daydreams and "tune out"—meaning that they are not paying attention in school or to their teachers. They lose points on tests because they do not read the directions. Children with this subtype often lose their belongings, are chronically late to appointments, and may struggle to get homework done because they "get lost" while trying to structure their time. As a result, even simple tasks wind up taking these children a great deal of time, as they tend to work inefficiently. At times, it can be taxing for these children to leave one activity and shift to another. For some, even leaving the house can be difficult, as they need to gather their belongings and shift their attention to a new set of tasks. Their lack of attention can even put them in harm's way; for instance, they may not notice passing cars or bikes while walking.

Socially, children with inattention problems are not usually seen as rude, but they may find it hard to relate to others. Peer relations, particularly in a group setting, may be difficult. While everyone is talking about one subject, these children may be speaking about another topic entirely, and while everyone on a sports team is running in one direction, they may run in another. As they get older, they may feel an acute sense of separation and may feel lonely as a result. They often thrive when relating to other kids one to one, rather than in a group.

Hyperactivity/Impulsivity

Children with hyperactivity and impulsivity have a constant need for action. As such, they are often physically restless, which makes them easier to recognize and diagnose with ADHD. Children with hyperactivity are particularly restless in tedious situations that do not involve stimulation or change. It may be difficult for them to slow down and take their time with any one thing. When they are young, they may move quickly from toy to toy, and when they're older, from activity to activity. When they find an activity that offers them stimulation, such as video games, they may "hyperfocus" on this activity and carry it out to the exclusion of everything else, including proper sleep, homework, and hygiene. They may find school tedious, except for areas of great interest, such as sports, drama, or any other activity that allows some degree of movement, freedom, and autonomy. These children may be classic underachievers in academic settings until they find a subject that stimulates their mind—and perhaps a mentor, role model, and/or teacher who inspires them.

Unfortunately, their impulsivity means that they can offend others socially and may run afoul of rules and social norms in school and at home. They often speak too much and do not filter what they say at times. They may be willing to engage in risky behavior to satisfy their need for stimulation or to win the attention of others. It's not unusual to find them playing the class clown; they fit naturally into the role of joking and talking, and their behavior also accomplishes the task of getting away from the work they find boring by distracting the teacher.

THE ADHD ADVANTAGE

ADHD presents unique challenges, but the ability to think creatively is not one of them. In fact, creativity may be more enhanced in children with ADHD. Many successful entertainers, such as actor and comedian Jim Carrey and musician Adam Levine, have ADHD. Levine has been quoted in ADDitude as saying, "ADHD isn't a bad thing, and you shouldn't feel different from those without ADHD." Nevertheless, people with ADHD often see the world in a different light, and may find inspiration in creative pursuits such as music, writing, acting, and other arts.

CHAPTER 3

Practical and Loving Parenting

Parenting a child with ADHD requires flexibility, invention, and a great deal of patience, not only with your child but also with yourself. While you will go on to help your child using the strategies this book discusses, it is important to realize that ADHD requires long-term management. Yes, the symptoms will improve, but the disorder will not just go away overnight. In some cases, it can be a lifelong condition. So, think of being the parent of a child with ADHD as an exciting adventure with myriad challenges, opportunities ... and happy surprises!

Take Mariah, a doctor. Her child, Jackson, was diagnosed with ADHD, and Mariah found it difficult to understand and empathize with his behaviors. He was clearly very bright, but he did not do the work expected of him and performed poorly in middle school. In high school, he discovered the magic of physics, and understood the subject so well that he excelled in it. But even though Mariah did not always relate to what Jackson was interested in, she acknowledged and accepted that he was going to do things in a very different way than she had. While Mariah went directly to medical school after college, Jackson decided to move to rural Maine for several years to work as an organic farmer. At the same time, he took pre-med courses and eventually enrolled in a scientific research graduate program several years after graduating from college. Along the way, he made friends with a disparate group of people, learned how to farm, and brought real-life knowledge to his study of science.

Like Jackson, many children with ADHD make surprising choices. If parents stay flexible and open-minded, however, they can support and guide their children as they make exciting discoveries about their own talents and interests.

When Parents Also Have ADHD

If you also have ADHD, it may make parenting your child with ADHD feel doubly hard, but your experiences may also make you more understanding and receptive to what your child is going through. In the last several years, the world of ADHD has changed a lot. There is a much greater understanding of the condition and strategies, medications, and other interventions that help children with ADHD perform better at school and at home. And since many more children are properly diagnosed now than in years past, they can receive the help they need.

Some adults with ADHD may not have been diagnosed when they were younger, and they may have grown up without understanding ADHD or having others around them understand what they were going through. If you can relate to this, be aware that your child's experiences will most likely be different from yours; there is a greater appreciation and understanding of ADHD today. You don't need to worry that your child's experiences will replicate your own. It is certainly helpful to self-reflect, but you'll want to avoid projecting any negativity from your past onto your child. The condition may be the same, but each individual is different.

If you grew up with ADHD, you likely have a greater sensitivity to your child's challenges and experiences. You may also be aware that there are benefits to having the condition. In fact, you can use your own sense of experimentation and flexibility to try out and adapt strategies to help your child. (Also, be sure to check out chapter 8 for some strategies you might like to try for yourself.)

Parenting Principles

As you help your child develop strategies to work with ADHD, there are several principles to keep in mind. These principles will help you guide your child in a realistic and caring way, with an understanding that there is no cure-all for ADHD. The guidance you provide can help your child work at their own pace toward understanding the condition and working with it.

THE ADHD ADVANTAGE

David Neeleman, an entrepreneur who started three commercial airlines, including JetBlue, has spoken publicly about growing up with ADHD. He dropped out of college and went on to found Morris Air, which was later sold to Southwest Airlines. Neeleman used his restlessness and sense of adventure to his advantage. He constantly rode on his own airplanes, making sure they were comfortable and engaging to his customers. He's the smart guy who decided to install TV screens into the back of each seat because he understood that people needed to be entertained as they flew. Having ADHD made him more inventive and, in part, helped him rethink the way a commercial airline treats its customers.

- **Practice patience:** All parents need patience, and this quality is particularly important for parents of children with ADHD. While it is natural for parents to want to "solve" their children's problems and "cure" their ADHD, the reality for most children is that they need time to develop. Studies conducted by the NIMH and others have shown that children with ADHD will develop in similar ways as that of their peers, except in brain development, where they lag behind about three years. These studies suggest that parents can be assured that their children will eventually develop the necessary organizational, planning, and judgment skills exercised by children without ADHD. But, the slower trajectory toward maturation means extra patience and an eye on long-term development, rather than quick fixes, may be necessary.

- **Keep an eye on the long term:** This is related to patience. Parents should understand that even though they are taking steps to help their child, they might not see immediate results. Change and maturation require time, and children may develop more slowly in some areas than in others. They may experience occasional setbacks, but these bumps in their development do not mean that they won't eventually have all of the tools they require for a rich and productive life.

- **Ask others for help:** While it is natural for parents to want to help their children on their own, it really does "take a village" to raise all kids, particularly those with learning differences. In other words, reach out to a community of people who have children with ADHD, whether online or in your area, for advice and support. It is a positive reflection of your parenting style to enlist the help of adults your child interacts with, including not only teachers but also perhaps coaches, tutors, doctors, therapists, and religious leaders. Enlisting the help of others may be particularly important as your child enters adolescence, a period when children are often less receptive to what their parents have to say.

■ **Externalize rewards:** As ADHD expert Russell Barkley, PhD, noted in *Taking Charge of ADHD*, children with ADHD may not internalize motivation as other children do over time, and they may need external motivations and supports to change their behavior. This does not mean that parents need to bribe children, but it does mean that parents need to consider what children with ADHD value, such as playing video games or sports, and use these interests as rewards for children's completion of more mundane activities. While many parents want children to carry out tasks just because it is the right thing to do, children with ADHD may need to be externally motivated until they can develop a more intrinsic sense of what they need to do over time. Several strategies in this book suggest external rewards to keep your child motivated.

■ **Recognize positive behaviors:** Children with ADHD often require constant feedback. Be sure to recognize what your child is doing well, even if it's just part of a larger task or something trivial. For example, while most school-age children can get dressed and eat breakfast independently, many children with ADHD need to be praised for each step of the process they complete on their own—for instance, putting on their socks or tying their shoes without help, or sitting at the table for ten minutes without fidgeting. Though many parents may feel that children should not be praised for tasks that are expected of them at a certain age, children with ADHD need this praise to motivate them to keep completing these tasks on their own. It may feel strange to praise children who are still developing skill sets that their peers have already incorporated—or which parents think are easy—but it is necessary to keep children with ADHD moving toward independence. Big leaps can happen in very unexpected time frames, and little changes happen all the time; be unconditionally supportive of your child, and notice when they succeed regardless of how trivial the accomplishment may seem to you.

- **Break down tasks and directions into smaller parts:** Children with ADHD often need longer tasks and directions broken down into smaller, easier to manage pieces. Parents, teachers, and other caregivers should avoid assuming that a child with ADHD will understand how to break down longer tasks on their own. For example, in the morning, your child may need a list of each task they need to complete. An example might look like this: (1.) Take your clothes out of your drawer. (2.) Put on your clothes starting with your socks, etc. School assignments need to be broken down similarly. Also, specific times for completion need to be assigned, as many children with ADHD do not have an intrinsic sense of how to plan or complete tasks within a certain time frame.

- **Communicate with teachers and other professionals:** Be open and honest with your child's teachers and other adults who work with your child, such as camp counselors. Children with ADHD have a legal right to special accommodations at school, including an Individualized Education Program (IEP), to help them succeed. However, many parents attempt to conceal an ADHD diagnosis, fearing that their child will be stigmatized. If they are not aware of the diagnosis, teachers and others in teaching and caregiving roles may assume a child is being willfully defiant or disruptive. If you communicate honestly about what your child is facing, this information will help teachers work with your child. Parents should not ask teachers to excuse their children from assignments. Instead, they should strategize with teachers about how to help their child complete the schoolwork.

- **Avoid comparing children to others, including siblings:** It can sometimes be difficult for parents who have children with different needs and developmental trajectories not to compare their children to their siblings or peers. Children with ADHD already have an acute sense of not measuring up, and these types of comparisons, when shared with children, do not tend to motivate them. Comparisons for the purpose of trying to show your child with ADHD how they should behave can frustrate them further and lead to less self-confidence in working toward developing the skills they need.

- **Keep in mind the particular challenges of girls with ADHD:** While all children with ADHD may find that their symptoms interfere with positive social interactions, girls with ADHD may run afoul of cultural stereotypes about the ways they should behave. For example, they may be considered odd, socially distractible, too brusque, bossy, or other qualities that society—including many children, parents, and teachers—are not taught to celebrate in girls. If you have a daughter with ADHD, read the strategy in chapter 6 on page 106 for helpful suggestions and resources.

- **Take advantage of ADHD's benefits and energy:** While there is no doubt that ADHD presents challenges, it also can confer a great sense of creativity, high energy, and often considerable charm. The old adage, "feed the hungry bee," is a good mantra for parents. Find what your child likes to do, and encourage them to do it. For example, let's say your child loves working with tools or taking things apart. Buy them a building set, perhaps, and see if your child might want to help you fix things around the house. In other words, find the activities and tasks they enjoy (or at least tolerate), and give them an out if there's a task they truly dislike. Who knows, given the choice, your child might discover a knack for folding laundry or thrive at the responsibility of ironing shirts!

- **Recognize and channel kids' interests:** As mentioned previously, many children with ADHD have specialized areas of interest they can develop. For example, they may have difficulty completing their homework, but they might be motivated by sports, drama, or robotics. You can help your child develop skills in an area of high interest, and your child will be more motivated to develop independence and discipline in that area. For example, if your child enjoys singing, they might set a goal of performing at a school concert, and you can help them develop a practice regimen. This experience can help your child understand the importance of hard work and breaking down preparation over time into small, achievable steps. Your child might then be more willing to internalize these lessons when completing traditional homework.

- **Take personal time to recuperate:** Parents of children with ADHD may simply feel exhausted, disappointed, and even isolated at times. They need to remember to take good care of themselves, too. If possible, find time to yourself to reflect and just relax. You might also enjoy joining groups for parents of children with ADHD so you can share experiences and strategies with others who are going through similar experiences. Connecting with other parents who understand what you are going through can also help reduce any sense of isolation you might be feeling.

Communicating Effectively with Your Child

When you communicate with your child, you will need to make sure that you are clearly and consistently presenting your demands, rules, and requests. Although it may sometimes be difficult to find, having patience is essential here. Children with ADHD may not have developed an internal sense of how they are expected to behave, so they need to be reminded of their tasks and often encouraged to complete these tasks with external motivators.

Make requests of your child in clear ways, broken down into simple parts. For example, some parents may need to make a list of each task their child needs to complete in the morning when getting ready for school. Other parents may need to provide clear reminders several times in advance that the child will be able to play only when their homework is completed.

Consequences need to be firmly communicated, as children benefit when rules and discipline are consistent. While it can be appealing to make exceptions, especially if a child is acting out, it is sometimes worse to upset the schedule. Depending on how your child learns, these types of changes can disrupt a developing sense of responsibility. Children may need external rewards to carry out their tasks until they internalize what they need to do. These don't have to be extravagant items—something like popcorn is a good reward before, after, or during your child's tasks. Try sitting with your child while they do homework to get them in a pattern of comfort with responsibility.

Children with ADHD often require advance notice of what they need to do so they can prepare. It can be ineffective to make immediate demands of them and then get angry when they are not carried out. Instead, you may need to think ahead of time about the rules or steps that children need to follow in general, and then build in additional time for your child with ADHD to complete these tasks.

If your child does not follow through on their responsibilities, gently remind your child of the consequence and enact it very quickly. For example, this may entail taking away a toy or turning off the television. Children with ADHD need to see immediate consequences of their actions, or they may not understand what the results of their actions are. Far-off or vague consequences do not work as well as immediate consequences. Always refrain from making personal or insulting comments, as many children with ADHD suffer from low self-confidence and a lack of self-worth. Instead, the consequences for not following through with what they need to do should be something tangible. Children with ADHD need to believe that their parents will consistently and fairly apply the consequences they spoke about in advance.

As children grow older, parents can begin to speak to them more openly about what having ADHD means. They can talk about what ADHD is, using age-appropriate language, and make it clear to children that they have a condition that requires them to develop strategies to work with it and around it. ADHD should not be presented as a weakness or as a failure, but simply as part of their particular learning style and the way they relate to the world, which requires them to be more inventive and perhaps work harder in certain ways than their peers. Medical professionals, such as psychologists and therapists, can also help children develop an awareness of having ADHD and what it means for their lives and coping styles. There is more information about helping children understand ADHD, age-appropriately, in part 2.

CHAPTER 4

Helping Your Child Thrive

You play a vital role in helping your child with ADHD reach their full potential. Today, there is help available on several fronts, including medication, alternative therapies, and strategies to help children manage their ADHD at home and at school. This chapter will help you begin to put together a treatment plan customized for your child's needs.

Working with Others on a Treatment Plan

Although you may want to take on the entire load of helping your child on your own, it is typically necessary to work with a team to help your child thrive. This team may include, at times, doctors, psychiatrists, psychologists, therapists, behaviorists, teachers, and other professionals. While it may seem overwhelming to work with so many people, each professional has a role to play in helping your child. You may not necessarily need all of them, but it is good to know how they might be able to assist you and your child.

First, your child may qualify for educational rights covered by the Americans with Disabilities Act (ADA) and the Individuals with Disabilities Education Act (IDEA). You can request an Individualized Education Program (IEP), which, as the name implies, is a specific, customized education plan tailored to the needs of your child. In a perfect world, every school would have a great special education program, but you may have to advocate for your child to the school administration to get what your child needs.

An IEP takes into account not only a child's strengths, but also recognizes that the child has a need for specific learning and development goals and identifies those goals. Ideally, there will be procedures to evaluate if those needs are being met. Your child also may have the right to special accommodations, such as extended time for standardized tests or the ability to use audiobooks or other devices. You can consult the Department of Education for more information (see the Resources section on page 150 for their website).

It is imperative to check in regularly with the professionals who are working with your child, and to be open and honest with them. For example, you should report, as objectively as possible, the behaviors you are seeing your child exhibit at home. In certain cases, medication dosages, treatment plans, or learning goals may need to be adjusted. Regular check-ins with your child's team are also necessary to ensure that their treatments are up to date. Make sure your child's doctor knows about any side effects you are noticing, as some can be serious. If you decide to discontinue a particular therapy or medication, be sure to share this information with your team, rather than acting on your own. Medication usually needs to be tapered off under the supervision of a doctor. You can also ask your child to keep an age-appropriate diary with impressions of the therapies, which can help them foster a sense of independence, while providing helpful information.

The truth is, it can be difficult at times to receive and implement feedback from so many different people. Ask friends or school

personnel for recommendations of professionals who h
fully treated other children with ADHD. If you feel tha
communicate openly with someone on your child's trea
or that they are pushing one particular type of treatmen
seem to be effective, try to find someone you can work with more
cohesively. This does not mean that the other person will always
say what you want to hear, but there are many paths to treatment.
Physicians, therapists, and learning specialists should always be open
to adapting their treatments to your child's specific needs. There is no
one-size-fits-all treatment. Make sure your team has time to speak
to you outside of sessions with your child to ensure that they are
getting the most complete information from you and you from them.

Medication

Only a qualified doctor can help you choose a medication for your
child. The doctor you work with should be experienced in working
with children with ADHD. If your child has coexisting conditions,
which were discussed in chapter 1, the doctor should be experienced
in treating those conditions as well. This section will acquaint you
with some common medications given to children with ADHD, as
well as their side effects, but it is not intended to replace the advice
of a qualified doctor about the right medication for your child.

Some medications work immediately, while others take some
time to show effects. In addition, at first, the medication may have the
reverse effect on your child; it may make some children seem more
agitated until their bodies adjust to it. While the effort to find the right
medication for your child can be somewhat anxiety producing, keep in
mind that psychiatry for children usually involves some experimentation and a period of adjustment—not just the dosage, but sometimes
different medication or a combination of medications. In the process,
share with your child's doctor any side effects you are seeing. Keep a
diary of your child's feelings or actions and, as mentioned previously,
ask your child to do the same at an age-appropriate level.

A doctor should not just prescribe medication without establishing a structure of follow-up appointments, so your team should be checking back in with you and your child regularly. In addition, the doctor may want to provide you and your child's teachers with forms to fill out inquiring about your child's symptoms; this information could be used to understand the efficacy of the treatment.

Amphetamine Stimulants

Amphetamine is thought to work as a treatment in ADHD by increasing the level of the neurotransmitter dopamine. People with ADHD naturally have lower levels of this neurotransmitter and, through stimulant therapy, this dopamine boost may have the effect of calming and focusing the minds of people with ADHD. The two main forms of amphetamine prescribed for ADHD are Adderall (mixed amphetamine salts) and Dexedrine (dextroamphetamine). They are generally prescribed as short-acting tablets and work over about four to six hours, meaning that some children will need to take another dose or part of a dose in the afternoon. There are some longer-acting (extended-release, or XR) versions of these medications that last about eight to twelve hours, including Adderall XR, Dexedrine XR, and Vyvanse (lisdexamfetamine). Some of the side effects associated with this class of medication include loss of appetite, weight loss, sleep loss, tics, anger, and irritable behavior. However, these side effects do not occur in all children who take these drugs. Some children and adults may find it easier to take non-time-release pills once they are familiar with the medicine's effect.

Methylphenidate Stimulants

Drugs in this class contain methylphenidate, a central nervous system stimulant, and include medications such as Focalin and Ritalin. Many are short acting, lasting about four to six hours, but extended-release versions are also available. Shorter-lasting medications may require additional doses during the day. The side effects associated with this class of medication include appetite loss, insomnia, weight loss, irritability, and tics. Some medications, such as the Daytrana patch, deliver the drugs through the skin and into the bloodstream without going through the digestive system. Children who use this type of patch do not need to swallow pills or visit their school nurses for afternoon doses. The patch can have similar side effects as other methylphenidate stimulants, and may cause skin irritation.

Nonstimulants

This class of drug does not contain amphetamines. The most common ones are Strattera (atomoxetine), which works by increasing norepinephrine, which regulates attention, and therefore decreases impulsivity and hyperactivity, and Intuniv (guanfacine) acting on receptors of the brain to improve attention, working memory, and control of impulses while decreasing distractibility. Common side effects associated with Strattera include insomnia, fatigue, anxiety, upset stomach, dizziness, dry mouth, and, in rare cases, liver damage. There is some concern Strattera may increase suicidal thoughts. Intuniv can cause sleepiness, fatigue, headaches, stomach pain, and, in rare cases, low blood pressure and changes in heart rhythm.

Antidepressants

Antidepressants such as Wellbutrin (bupropion) are available in short-acting and longer-acting forms, and they are sometimes given to children with ADHD. Wellbutrin can result in sleep problems, headaches, and, rarely, seizures. Sometimes, children who cannot tolerate stimulant medication or who suffer from tics or insomnia are prescribed antidepressants to reduce symptoms of inattention, impulsivity, and hyperactivity.

Blood Pressure Medications

Certain blood pressure medications, including clonidine, are sometimes given to children with ADHD. Clonidine can be taken alone or in combination with stimulant medication to reduce ADHD symptoms, and it may also reduce aggression and the insomnia associated with stimulant medication. Clonidine can cause fatigue, dizziness, irritable behavior, low blood pressure, and dry mouth.

While taking medication can help children reduce the symptoms associated with ADHD, medication does not cure ADHD. Instead, the right medication at the proper dose can help a child remain more focused, reduce hyperactivity, and curb impulsivity so that they can attend to everyday tasks as well as adhere to strategies that can further help them be productive. So, in other words, medications are best when combined with learning and psychological interventions aimed at helping a child develop strategies to plan, organize, and learn effectively. Consult Russell A. Barkley's book, *Taking Charge of ADHD*, for more information about medication for children with ADHD.

ADHD DRUG ABUSE

Many people, particularly students in high school and college, take stimulant medication that is not prescribed to them in the mistaken belief that it will improve their performance or ability to learn. People who do not have ADHD who take these medications do not show an enhanced ability to learn, and they can pose serious side effects and complications if taken without a prescription and without the care of a doctor. Young people who take these medications should be told that sharing medication is illegal and potentially dangerous. This is discussed further in chapter 7.

MANAGING COMMON SIDE EFFECTS FROM MEDICATION

Many medications that treat ADHD can pose some common side effects, including insomnia, weight loss, loss of appetite, and anxiety. If your child is experiencing these side effects (or any of the others mentioned in the previous sections), stay in touch with your child's prescribing physician on a regular basis. Let the doctor know what is going on by keeping detailed daily records of your child's behavior and symptoms, and make sure your child sees the doctor regularly.

To counteract the negative effects of medication, your child's doctor might change the dosage of the medication or prescribe new medication. For example, some children need to take a second dose of stimulant medication in the afternoon, when the morning dose is wearing off and causing irritability or loss of attention. Be aware that getting the right dose of medication can take several weeks or even months of experimentation. In other words, psychiatry is not an exact science. This type of trial-and-error period does not mean that the prescribing doctor is incompetent. While this process may be difficult for you and your child, reassure your child (and yourself!) that every child is different, and that it can take some time to find the right dose.

Once your child finds what works for them, the doctor may allow them to take days or weeks off from the medication, such as on weekends or during the summer, which may lessen the medication's side effects while still allowing your child to take it when needed to reduce the symptoms of inattention, hyperactivity, and impulsivity (such as on days when they are taking tests, etc.).

As your child grows, their medications may need to be changed, as some medications may lose their effectiveness over time. Your child's changing body might also require different types or doses of medication, and your child may again need to go through a period of experimentation. During this trial period, your child's new medications or doses may pose different side effects that again need to be brought to the doctor's attention and monitored.

Alternative Therapies

Some children with ADHD have benefited from alternative therapies, and you may find the same is true for your child. It is just a matter of trying them out to see what works. Though there is a general lack of scientific research behind these types of therapy, there is a good deal of anecdotal information that many of these treatments are helpful. As with any therapy, give it sufficient time for the benefits to kick in. When you work with a professional in these areas, they will be able to advise you on how long you may need to wait to see results.

Modified Diets

While sugar has long been named a culprit in *causing* ADHD, there is little science that backs up this claim. However, sugar and refined carbohydrates, such as white flour products, can increase children's activity levels by causing a rush of sugar into the bloodstream. Also, many people with ADHD (adults and children alike) tend to self-medicate with sugary snacks, and if you or your child has this habit, it's best to nip it in the bud immediately. The adrenaline spike that results from a sugar rush can cause children to act in a more hyperactive way, even if they are on medication to counter this. All children, not just those with ADHD, can benefit from a balanced diet to keep their blood sugar steady over the course of the day. A diet that includes fruits, vegetables, and whole grain products, such as oatmeal and whole wheat bread, is good for children's general health.

Some parents have experienced success placing their children on the Feingold diet, which was developed by allergist Benjamin Feingold, MD. He advocates eliminating foods containing artificial dyes, flavorings, and preservatives from the diet to reduce hyperactivity. While the Feingold diet has not been supported by scientific studies, some parents believe it has resulted in reduced hyperactivity in their children.

Research has shown that children with ADHD may have a decreased level of omega-3 fatty acids in their blood and that they can benefit from supplements. In controlled studies conducted with an experimental and placebo group, children with ADHD showed a small but significant reduction in symptoms.

Parents will sometimes use an elimination diet to rule out foods that may exacerbate their children's ADHD symptoms. This diet, in which certain types of food are eliminated or added at particular intervals and effects then measured, can identify likely culprits that affect a child's behavior. If you are interested in trying an elimination diet, work with your child's doctor and a nutritionist to ensure that your child is still eating a well-balanced diet in the process.

Cognitive Behavioral Therapy for ADHD

Although first developed to help people cope with depression and anxiety, cognitive behavioral therapy (CBT) can help people with ADHD learn to change the thoughts and behaviors that may worsen their ADHD symptoms and that lead to disorganization and poor time management. People undergoing CBT often meet in groups with a therapist to work on issues such as organizational and time-management skills. Participants involved in these group programs have shown improvements compared to those in traditional supportive therapies. These types of programs work best with older, more verbal, children and adults. One-on-one CBT therapy sessions are also an option.

Neurofeedback

Some people with ADHD have tried neurofeedback training with success. This biofeedback technique allows a person to monitor their own brain activity through sensors placed on their head, which send audio or visual signals to a monitoring device. The idea is that by developing this awareness, patients can eventually learn to regulate their own brain activity. However, many believe research is necessary to determine the effectiveness of this type of training for ADHD. Also, be aware that neurofeedback can be expensive and time-intensive.

Working Memory Training (COGMED)

Some people with ADHD have issues with their working memory, which can interfere with carrying out memory-related tasks. Working memory is the transient memory that holds and stores incoming information; it is the ability to hold information in the mind for a short period and use it until the information is transferred to long-term memory. Working memory plays an important role in learning and in mentally manipulating symbols and other cognitive functions. COGMED training involves using a computer program to increase one's working memory capability and capacity and to improve concentration and problem-solving skills. Studies have demonstrated some short-term improvements in working memory, though so far, the results suggest that only visual memory is increased over the long term with this type of therapy.

Meditation

Some people with ADHD may rely on the rush of adrenaline that comes with feeling very stimulated to rouse themselves to action. For example, they may only be able to work on tasks when they can no longer procrastinate, resulting in a stress reaction that propels them into action. However, this constant flood of adrenaline has a negative effect on both the body and the mind. It can cause wear and tear on anyone and may result in lowered immunity.

To counteract this, a person with ADHD may benefit from meditation to calm their body and mind. While it may be difficult to introduce children—especially younger ones—to sitting in silence, anyone can be trained in simple techniques over time, such as repeating a mantra with their eyes closed or concentrating on the intake or exhalation of their breath. They may need a focus object, such as a toy or favorite stuffed animal, to help them concentrate their mind and vision. If meditation is something you think may benefit your child, meditate with your child, and ask them what feels most relaxing and comforting for them. Sometimes, very creative children benefit from specific visualization techniques, in which they go on an imaginary, relaxing adventure.

If a child cannot sit still, they may be better able to meditate following yoga or light exercise like walking. They may enjoy meditating outside in a peaceful place such as near the ocean or lake or in a clearing in the woods. They can start by paying attention to the sensory input around them, such as the calls of birds or the waves, to start to focus and calm their minds. To find more ideas about how to visualize while meditating, check out Project Meditation, which is listed in the Resources section on page 151.

Equine Therapy

Some children with ADHD benefit from equine-assisted psychotherapy. This type of therapy incorporates horses into a treatment program aimed at assisting an individual in reaching certain goals. While learning to ride a horse, the child observes the horse's moods and learns the horse's needs, thereby becoming less focused on themselves and better able to understand how their actions affect others. Equine-assisted psychotherapy usually involves debriefing with a counselor following one's interaction with the horse to build self-awareness. Some studies have shown that by interacting with horses and learning how one's behavior affects them, children can experience a reduction of their symptoms of inattention, hyperactivity, and impulsivity. Children often relate well to horses, because horses react without judgment or criticism—and make their needs easily known. Combined with this instant and observable feedback lesson, children may also feel more confident knowing that they can help guide a powerful animal like a horse. This type of therapy has also shown to reduce anxiety and depression.

QUIZ: WHAT ARE YOUR CHILD'S ADHD CHALLENGES?

This quiz will help you pinpoint your child's specific challenges and refine your understanding of the types of issues they are facing so that you can find the most effective strategies to help them. Check the behaviors that apply to your child based on frequency, and use this information in your child's treatment plan.

1. My child is often restless. YES ☐ NO ☐ SOMETIMES ☐

2. My child daydreams constantly. YES ☐ NO ☐ SOMETIMES ☐

3. My child is angry or explosive. YES ☐ NO ☐ SOMETIMES ☐

4. My child loses belongings. YES ☐ NO ☐ SOMETIMES ☐

5. My child is prone to injury. YES ☐ NO ☐ SOMETIMES ☐

6. My child loses track of time. YES ☐ NO ☐ SOMETIMES ☐

7. My child speaks out of turn. YES ☐ NO ☐ SOMETIMES ☐

8. My child cannot keep up with conversations. YES ☐ NO ☐ SOMETIMES ☐

9. My child struggles with insomnia. YES ☐ NO ☐ SOMETIMES ☐

10. My child is always lagging behind others. YES ☐ NO ☐ SOMETIMES ☐

If you answered "yes" or "sometimes" to many of the odd-numbered statements, your child may be contending with impulsivity and hyperactivity. The plan you develop for your child should include ways to calm their mind and channel their energy productively. You will need to build in time for your child to be active. Also, be realistic about how much your child can pay attention during more sedentary or tedious activities. Your child might be very inventive and have the energy to explore new possibilities.

If you answered "yes" or "sometimes" mostly to the even-numbered statements, your child may be primarily contending with inattention. Your plan will be focused on helping your child attend and keep track of time, belongings, and other activities. Your child may need to build in quiet daily activities that do not overwhelm them. Your child might be a creative person who uses times of inattention to daydream and create art, stories, or other inventions.

If you answered "yes" or "sometimes" to both the odd and even statements, your child may be contending with inattention, hyper-activity, and impulsivity. In this case, your plan will need to address ways to help your child be more attentive while reducing or channeling hyperactivity and impulsivity. Your child might be a creative person who has a lot of energy and the potential to make their inventive ideas a reality.

NOTE: This quiz is intended to help you identify some of your child's behaviors that you would like to address and work on through the strategies presented in part 2 of this book. It is not intended to be diagnostic or to replace an evaluation by a doctor or psychologist. If you are looking for that type of information, please ask your doctor or psychologist to explain your child's diagnosis in greater detail. If a psychologist evaluated your child, the psychoeducational evaluation the psychologist provides can offer you very nuanced and detailed information about how your child's mind works. If you find the evaluation difficult to understand, make an appointment with the psychologist to go over the report and ask the psychologist to put the findings into a layperson's terms.

Modifying Your Parenting Approach

Using the feedback from the quiz, as well as what you know about your child, you can modify your parenting approach to take into account your child's strengths, challenges, interests, goals, and resources. Here's how:

First, assess your child's considerable strengths and remind yourself of all the great qualities your child brings to the table. For example, your child might be creative, insightful about other people, brave, athletic, or many other things. You can use these qualities in your parenting approach. If your child is insightful, they can use those skills to observe other people's coping strategies and see if they work for them, using their creativity.

Second, assess your child's challenges and what they need to work on. For example, your child may be inattentive, or have trouble completing homework and/or have trouble initiating tasks; they may also have difficulty getting along with peers, leading to moodiness.

Third, using your child's strengths and challenges, formulate some realistic goals that you and your child might be able to achieve within the next few months or so. For example, it might be realistic to have your child keep a homework log in a notebook, or on a computer or other device. To help them keep on track, simply write the starting time of each assignment and how long it took to complete the task. This will help you and your child create an achievable, measurable set of goals. If your child is outgoing, perhaps they can also sign up for an after-school study club to help them initiate their work.

Finally, consider what resources you will need to support your child. For example, if your child has trepidations about the social pressures of joining a homework club, they may be able to work with the school counselor or therapists (or other people on your team of helpers) on peer relations. Aside from the school and your ADHD support team, resources can include local community centers and groups, religious or social institutions, and ADHD support groups (see the Resources section on page 148 for more information).

Sample Parenting Approaches

Different children may require very different parenting approaches. Let's first consider Emily, a shy, inattentive ten-year-old with obvious talents. Emily is always writing poems and is a gifted and devoted reader, as well as a gentle person. Her challenges are that she contends with distractibility, and she leaves tasks unfinished or forgets to complete them. She often loses her backpack, scarves, and homework, and she has difficulty making friends and keeping up with the other kids at school. In class, she likes to contribute, but she can make comments that seem unrelated to other people's remarks, causing other kids to laugh at her. She is sensitive to criticism. Even mild-mannered suggestions from her parents and teachers can cause her to react strongly or cry.

A realistic approach for Emily involves constant spoken and written reminders of what she needs to do to keep her on track. It will be essential to use her interest and skills (in this case, her poetry) to keep her involved and motivated. For example, she can write a poem to remind herself of what she needs to accomplish that day, or do a ten-minute freewrite before beginning her homework to help her focus. Emily's parents should be sure to praise her achievements on a regular level and to respond to mistakes with redirection rather than criticism or yelling. If Emily wants to, she can join intramural clubs in school to make friends with other kids who enjoy writing or theater. And to make the best use of the resources available to their daughter, her parents should set up meetings with Emily's teachers to let them know more about Emily's needs—and to inform them that she wants to contribute to class discussions but does not always know how to do so. This approach can also be taken with the help of the school's special education department, which often acts as a liaison between parents and teachers.

Now let's consider Jake, an active nine-year-old who enjoys playing video games and swimming. He is a funny kid who loves delivering stand-up comedy routines and is very good at sports. He usually can't follow directions at home or at school, and he is generally restless and prone to injury. He tends to fidget in class, and he is often frustrated by activities that require sustained attention. Jake finds it difficult to regulate his moods, and he can become irritable. He can react to criticism with angry outbursts, and he often fights with his siblings.

A parenting approach for Jake will involve channeling and using his energy. He should be encouraged to continue swimming because the sport does not require constant directions and poses a low risk of injury. If Jake is motivated to do so, he could consider doing a morning swim at the local community center before school to quiet his mind and get out some of his energy. He will need to attend to homework and tasks that require more concentration after he has been active, or he won't be able to complete them. He should be given clear and constant directions. If he reacts with anger to criticism, he needs to be given a safe space away from siblings to cool down. His parents should react as calmly as possible to his outbursts, as their anger will only escalate his behavior. His parents' approach should be to write out a list of activities that Jake needs to accomplish each afternoon and reward him with time playing video games if he finishes—and to stick to it. They can also set up a space for him in the basement with a basketball hoop and sign him up for morning swim at the local community center.

You may find it helpful to break down your parenting approach in the following way:

1. Your child's strengths
2. Your child's challenges
3. Realistic goals for you and your child to achieve in a reasonable amount of time
4. The resources needed to accomplish these goals

For example, here's how the parents of a nine-year-old fourth grader named Sydney might break down their parenting approach:

- **Strengths:** She is energetic, creative, and loves to play music.

- **Challenges:** She can, at times, be impulsive, speak out of turn, and melt down into rages when she feels people don't understand her. In addition, though she is bright, she struggles with the steps in math equations and with reading comprehension.

- **Goals:** In the next month, Sydney will start working with the after-school tutoring program at school, focusing on math and reading. Within the next two months, she will start meeting with a girls' ADHD support group. Using a star system, she will be rewarded by each teacher for each day that she does not interrupt, fight with peers, or get out of her seat. She can accumulate and trade these stars for breaks to play music during recess, for instance.

- **Resources:** Sydney will need to sign up for the after-school homework sessions at her school. Her parents will contact the local ADHD support group to find out the schedule for the girls' group. Sydney's teacher will come up with a behavior chart that tracks her progress in school.

The Supportive Family

While you may be eager to try a new parenting approach for your child, keep in mind that making changes often involves some successes along with inevitable failures. Enlist the child's siblings, relatives, and caregivers in the new approach so that your child can experience consistent reactions and discipline from everyone.

Be sure that your goals for yourself, your child, and the rest of your family are realistic. While every parent wants the best for their child and their families overall, keep in mind that lasting change happens over time. If you keep your goals achievable, measurable, and evolving, you, your child, and the rest of the family will stay motivated. Plan for the next few months instead of setting goals that are so lofty you will lose steam before you can see them come to fruition.

It can sometimes be difficult to get your other children to cooperate with your plans to help your child with ADHD. They may feel resentful that their sibling gets what may be perceived as more attention from you and other people. In this case, be sure to build in rewards and attention for their efforts to support your parenting plan for your child with ADHD. Also, be aware that children often become comfortable in certain roles within the family. Your other children may react negatively or resentful toward their sibling with ADHD as that child seeks to change their behaviors and place in the family. You can counter this by clearly communicating to the whole family that, regardless of any changes that take place, everyone has a special place in the family. Reward small successes along the way toward change and celebrate together as a family. The path may be bumpy and slow, but you will arrive on the other side!

PART TWO

Targeted Strategies for Managing ADHD

The chapters that follow present age-appropriate strategies for parenting a child with ADHD. These strategies are intended to help you develop a realistic parenting plan. If you also have ADHD, you may find the information in chapter 8 particularly helpful to you as well. Some of the strategies involve techniques you can implement yourself, while others involve getting help from other sources, including doctors, therapists, teachers, and community organizations. Each strategy includes the following:

- **Targeted challenge:**
  Lists relevant ADHD issue(s)
- **Overview:**
  Provides context for the strategy
- **Strategy implementation:**
  Lists ways to put the strategy into action
- **Long-term considerations:**
  Notes additional information that may be relevant later
- **Helpful modifications and tools:**
  Shares tips for adapting the strategy to different needs

CHAPTER 5

Preschool-Age Children

(AGE 5 AND UNDER)

This chapter will present some strategies that you can use with children under age six. Diagnosing ADHD in children under the age of six is still controversial. Most of the diagnostic criteria for ADHD are based on a school setting, such as being out of one's chair, so it can make it difficult to diagnose ADHD in other settings. While some experts believe that children younger than six should not be conclusively diagnosed with ADHD, others feel that they have refined the diagnostic procedure to the point where they can reliably diagnose children as young as age four.

Many preschool-age children have high energy and difficulty controlling their impulses, and these behaviors may be completely aligned with typical development. Some children of this age are in daycare or preschool programs that emphasize sitting and direct instruction, which may not be developmentally appropriate or recommended for them. In fact, kids this age learn a great deal by playing, and they should have the freedom to be physically active and to experiment with toys and play freely. In other words, many of the behaviors that children of this age show can present like ADHD, and so it can be hard to tell whether these symptoms present enough impairment to meet the criteria for the ADHD diagnosis.

In addition, some other disorders or conditions can look like ADHD in children of this age. For example, children with high-functioning autism or pervasive developmental disorder (PDD) may have similar forms of distractibility to kids with ADHD, but the causes of these symptoms are different. Other children have sensory issues that make it hard for them to sit still or attend to tasks, and others have anxiety, depression, mood disorders, or other conditions that make them seem inattentive or impulsive. However, ADHD may not be at the root of their behavior. It is essential to not label children at this age, but to simply be aware of their behaviors and monitor them.

If your child has not been diagnosed with ADHD, but you are reading this book because you believe that your child has much higher activity levels or seems more distractible than their peers, consult a doctor or psychologist who has experience working with children with ADHD. This is not a simple diagnosis. According to the *DSM-5* guidelines, symptoms must have been present before the age of twelve (in the *DSM-4*, it was age seven) for doctors or psychologists to diagnose ADHD. Therefore, it can be tricky to conclusively diagnose children younger than age six or seven.

Nevertheless, the main reason to have your child diagnosed early is to make sure treatment starts early. An early diagnosis of ADHD means that children can get the services they need before they start kindergarten. In addition, research has suggested that early treatment can help reduce symptoms over time. If your child has been diagnosed with ADHD at a very young age, be sure to revisit the diagnosis if you notice changes as your child ages. Many other conditions, as mentioned previously, can be interpreted as ADHD.

The following are some strategies that can help your preschool-age child who has been diagnosed with ADHD (or who is suspected by a professional of having the condition) to get the most enjoyment and productivity out of their daily activities and tasks.

MAKE CHANGES IN CLASSROOM/ DAYCARE AND SOCIAL SETTINGS

Targeted Challenges: Helps children with inattention, hyperactivity, and impulsivity; helps them use their strengths to overcome obstacles in the school setting.

Overview: Children who are in a formal preschool or daycare setting can benefit from changes that may reduce their ADHD symptoms. These adjustments are the easiest and least expensive to make.

STRATEGY IMPLEMENTATION:

1. Look for schools or daycare settings that have small class sizes. They tend to have fewer distractions and less movement in the classroom. Also consider Montessori or other small school programs that are focused on the child's gifts and strengths, rather than on making them adhere to more formal classroom norms.

2. Request that your child be seated near the teacher or daycare instructor in activities such as meetings on the classroom rug or during story time.

Long-Term Considerations: Children with ADHD require constant monitoring to be sure that their classroom settings and placements are appropriate for them. Parents should check in regularly with teachers to monitor if the child is doing well. If small changes in their classroom or daycare settings do not work, they might need a classroom with even fewer children or with more teacher support.

Helpful Modifications and Tools: Choose social activities that typically involve fewer children. For example, your child might participate better in a swim, karate, gymnastics, or art class with fewer than ten children than in a soccer practice that involves thirty kids.

PROVIDE FREQUENT BREAKS WORKSHEET #1

Targeted Challenges: Helps children with the symptoms of distractibility and hyperactivity.

Overview: During preschool or daycare activities, children should be allowed to take breaks from the activities and have spaces to go to with less distraction. Being around other children for extended periods of time and having to participate in tedious or overly sedentary activities (many of which might be inappropriate for children of this age) will tend to worsen symptoms of distractibility and hyperactivity.

STRATEGY IMPLEMENTATION:

1. Provide breaks that restore your child's stimulation levels to an optimal level. For hyperactive children, give them a few minutes to walk or run off their energy every hour or so. For children who present with inattention, give them a break that employs a quieter activity, such as meditation, yoga, or listening to calming music.

2. Ask the preschool teacher or daycare staff to find your child a space where they can take a break to restore their optimal stimulation levels.

3. In public settings, such as a busy grocery store, provide breaks by letting your child listen to calming music on headphones, or by letting them stretch in a quiet place, away from heavily trafficked areas.

Continued

4. Keep in mind that your child may need breaks in places that are loud and overstimulating, such as birthday parties, play dates with several children, family gatherings, sports games, and some places of worship.

5. Your child may also need a break when shifting from one activity to another. For example, it can be a struggle for your child to decompress after a stimulating event such as the school day, a birthday party, or a noisy family dinner. Several different activities in one day may be too much for your child to handle. For example, a child with ADHD who returns from a friend's birthday party may have an outburst of anger or frustration if they are immediately expected to have a long, quiet dinner with family members. The child may need time alone to regroup or engage in an energy-channeling activity such as running in the backyard or playground, before shifting to the next activity.

Long-Term Considerations: Children of this age will need help selecting the right kinds of breaks, though as they get older, they may develop a better sense of how to calm themselves and restore their attention to productive levels.

> **Helpful Modifications and Tools:** Observe how different activities affect your child's activity level, and make a note of when your child is calm. Log this information in Worksheet #1. Also note which activities preceded these calm moments, as these activities are good clues for the best types of breaks for your child.

WORKSHEET #1: Activities and Break Time Log

When describing activities that affect your child's ADHD symptoms, try to include details that may be particularly useful to know, such as the number of people present or the intensity of the stimulation involved. Rate your child's hyperactivity and inattention on a scale of 1 to 10, with 1 indicating very calm or focused behavior and 10 indicating very hyperactive or inattentive behavior.

DAY & TIME	ACTIVITY DESCRIPTION	CHILD'S BEHAVIOR	SYMPTOMS RATING	CONCLUSION
Sun 3:00-3:45 pm	Quick trip to park; much more crowded than usual; extremely hot weather	More hyperactive than usual	8	Crowded parks do not generate calm.

PROVIDE CLEAR, SIMPLE DIRECTIONS

Targeted Challenges: Helps children with symptoms of inattention and distractibility.

Overview: Children with ADHD may not always attend to directions. At this age, most directions are oral rather than written. Parents, teachers, and other caregivers should provide directions in the clearest, simplest terms. Children with ADHD who do not follow directions may not be willfully disobedient; instead, their inattentive symptoms and distractibility may make it very difficult for them to marshal their resources and regulate their energy to complete tasks.

STRATEGY IMPLEMENTATION:

1. Break down instructions into small steps using clear, simple language.

2. Make sure the instructions are specific and concrete. For example, instead of telling your child, "Get ready to go to school," you can say, "First, go brush your teeth. Then, put on your clothes."

 Helpful Modifications and Tools: Spell out steps using pictures. Visual cues may help children who have a limited ability to pay attention to oral language at this age.

Use charts to help your child complete tasks, and give rewards when they are successful with their tasks. For example, they can have a chart on their wall of all the steps they need to follow when getting ready for school or getting ready for bed. Each step they complete can be rewarded with a star on the chart or verbal praise.

Ask teachers to use charts to help your child. For example, teachers might make a chart with pictures of what children need to do during each phase of the school day, with each step broken down. There might be a picture of a child getting their backpack, putting on their coat, sitting quietly, and then boarding a school bus.

TRY A PARENT TRAINING PROGRAM

Targeted Challenges: Helps parents develop methods to respond to the core symptoms of ADHD in their child.

Overview: Schools and ADHD support groups (listed in the Resources section on page 148) often offer parent training programs for parents of children with ADHD. Training should focus on helping parents reinforce positive behaviors and reduce negative behaviors in their children, as well as introduce early language and math skills.

STRATEGY IMPLEMENTATION:

1. Respond to your child's behaviors with positive reinforcement. Praise your child immediately for what they do right.

2. Respond to negative behaviors by offering consistent and immediate consequences such as the removal of or reduction in your child's time watching television.

3. Help your child develop age-appropriate early language and math skills in one-on-one settings to make sure they are getting the necessary exposure to early language.

4. Read to and with your child before the age of five. This will improve their vocabulary and facilitate their eventual ability to read.

5. Teach number and math skills by helping your child connect numbers to whatever their interests are. For example, if your child likes basketball, count as you shoot baskets so that your child identifies numbers with an enjoyable activity.

Helpful Modifications and Tools: If your parent training program is not providing you with the results you are looking for, try behavioral therapy (see Investigate Behavioral Therapy" on page 76).

MAKE HOME A SAFE SPACE

Targeted Challenges: Helps children develop more self-confidence and better self-esteem, and they feel more physically and emotionally safe and comfortable at home.

Overview: Children who may experience exclusion or misunderstanding outside the home need a safe space in their home where they can go to decompress.

STRATEGY IMPLEMENTATION:

1. Create a place in your home where your child can go to take a break away from siblings and other relatives.

2. Furnish this space with soft pillows and seating and decorate it with a relaxing palette of colors, particularly if your child tends to be hyperactive or gets overwhelmed easily.

   - Exclude electronics. While children with ADHD often enjoy watching television, playing video games, and using smartphones or tablets, break spaces should generally be free of stimulating electronics. However, a speaker should be in place so there is an opportunity for your child to listen to soothing music.

   - Include your child's favorite nonelectronic toys in this space, so that they will want to go there. If possible, provide some favorite snacks in the area.

3. Use this space as a tool to preempt or head off bad behavior when you notice your child's behavior is escalating toward a punishment. Take your child to this calming space before their behavior reaches the point at which a punishment is necessary.

4. While this space may be associated with time-outs, you want to make it enjoyable and acceptable to your child by also making it a place where they can play and relax. Don't send your child to this space only when they are showing negative behaviors. Instead, have your child play there when they are relaxed and able to have fun, so they associate it with positive rewards, not just negative consequences.

Long-Term Considerations: Children should experience home as a rewarding place, both physically and emotionally. They should know that home is a place where they will be held accountable for their actions, but must also be overtly assured they will be safe, comfortable, and recognized for their talents. As your child grows, you may need to update their special place to make it enjoyable and relevant to their current interests.

Helpful Modifications and Tools: Provide consequences for your child's negative actions; these consequences can include a time-out or removal from a favored activity.

Find opportunities for your child to do what they do best at home. For example, children who love to dress up can help a parent choose an outfit or children who like to fix things can help a parent make household repairs. Children will understand that parents are supporting their strengths and recognizing what they do well.

PROVIDE CONSTANT FEEDBACK AND FREQUENT PRAISE

Targeted Challenges: Helps children with impulsivity and inattention and helps them build confidence.

Overview: Children with ADHD respond to frequent feedback. They do not always have internalized senses of their responsibilities, and they often need external reminders and rewards, particularly at young ages, until they begin to internalize what is required of them. Along with breaking down complicated or multistep tasks to make them more easily digestible, parents should praise each step the child completes along the way.

STRATEGY IMPLEMENTATION:

1. Do not offer your child hollow or empty praise, such as "You're such a good girl." Children tend to tune out to repeated clichéd phrases over time.

2. Provide your child with concrete, specific praise such as, "I like the way you helped me set the table," or "Wow! You really reorganized the bookshelf in such a cool way!" Children will begin to associate praise with actual accomplishments that they will want to repeat.

3. Develop statements that reward your child for specific behaviors that can be replicated, rather than for overgeneralizations about their personality. For example, the following are some phrases you can use and adapt to praise your child:

   - "You did a very nice job at [whatever task]." (Rather than overgeneralized statements such as "You're so smart," or "You're such a great kid.")

   - "I like how kind you were to your friend by sharing."

- "Your picture is so colorful."

- "I like that you practiced using kind words, like 'please' and 'thank you.'"

- "You did a great job staying quiet during the activity today."

4. Develop statements that help your child understand that their behaviors have real effects on other people rather than over-generalize poor behavior. For example, the following are some phrases you can use to discipline your child:

- "Using words like that hurts my feelings [or those of another person]."

- "Not sharing with your friends makes them feel hurt and sad."

- "Yelling hurts my ears."

- "When you speak that way, it makes me feel sad."

- "When you speak so quickly, I can't understand you."

Long-Term Considerations: Over time, children should develop a more internalized sense of what they need to do and may not require so much praise or feedback.

Helpful Modifications and Tools: Make sure you are praising your child's behavior, not their personality or qualities. Research conducted by expert Carol Dweck of Stanford University and others suggests that general praise of a child's personality or appearance makes them more likely to feel worried that they will lose their parents' praise and love if they make a mistake. However, praise that is attached to a specific act makes children want to repeat that act without fearing that they will lose their parents' overall affection if they do something wrong.

SET UP A CONSISTENT BEDTIME ROUTINE

Targeted Challenges: Helps children with hyperactivity and improves self-regulation and self-stimulation.

Overview: Bedtime can be the most difficult part of the day for children with ADHD. Children with hyperactivity may find it difficult to wind down, and parents need to build in time for children to calm themselves after the day and prepare for sleep. Many children with ADHD also struggle with their sleep–wake cycle, making them sleepy during the daytime and awake at night. However, sleep is vitally important for developing minds and bodies, and the lack of sleep can worsen ADHD symptoms. Setting a consistent bedtime and bedtime ritual helps children's bodies adjust to a schedule and gives them enough time to relax before bed.

STRATEGY IMPLEMENTATION:

1. Establish a consistent bedtime, and stick to nighttime routines.

2. Start helping your child wind down with relaxing activities about an hour before the established bedtime.

3. Post a chart on your child's wall with pictures of the activities they will need to complete before going to bed (including brushing their teeth, changing into pajamas, reading a story, etc.).

4. Soothe your child by choosing comfortable toys to sleep with and selecting an activity, such as reading a book for about ten minutes, before bedtime. This helps with nighttime fears as well.

5. Avoid letting your child play video games, watch television, or use smartphones or tablets before bed. Aside from the obvious stimulation, the ambient light from these devices has been shown to keep the brain alert. Be sure to keep charging devices away from where children are sleeping, as devices still emit light when charging.

Long-Term Considerations: Help your child develop better sleep habits and practices (sometimes referred to as sleep hygiene). This will help them learn to recognize when they are tired and to follow the steps necessary for a good night's sleep. While preschoolers are in the very early stages of developing this type of awareness, as a parent, you can help identify calming pre-bedtime rituals and activities, and make modifications to their bedroom, such as playing soft music, providing a special blanket that helps them go to sleep, or installing a night-light. Make it a good, consistent pattern, and stick to it. Since adolescence can wreak havoc in growing children's sleep cycles, it is essential to help them develop good sleep hygiene at a young age. If children are consistently getting the sleep they need, they may experience a reduction in the core symptoms of ADHD.

Helpful Modifications and Tools: If your child is still struggling with bedtime or having issues staying asleep, you may want to consult your child's team or a naturopathic physician about safe homeopathic remedies (check for contraindications with other medications with your doctor first), or ask for a referral to a sleep specialist.

CREATE AN ADHD-FRIENDLY HOME

Targeted Challenges: Helps reduce hyperactivity and the risk of injury in the home.

Overview: ADHD-friendly houses often have soft, unbreakable objects and the types of storage that are easy to use, such as open bins or marked cubicles.

STRATEGY IMPLEMENTATION:

1. Create a system in which each toy has its own space and is not difficult to store. For example, you can install open storage bins in play areas into which your child can dump toys without much thought.

2. Clearly label your child's belongings with their name and possibly your phone number, particularly if these objects are going to school, daycare, or camp.

3. Create open areas where your child can run and play at home without bumping into objects.

4. Find ways your child can get exercise without leaving home or the yard. Ask your child what they are most interested in exploring, and find ways to make it happen in a safe way.

5. Furnish your home with sturdy furniture that is not easily tipped over, broken, or stained. Secure heavy items such as bookcases by fastening them down or to the wall. This will reduce the risk of injuries caused by children climbing on furniture.

Long-Term Considerations: Children should develop safe ways to channel their energy. They should be able to be active in the home in a manner that does not pose a risk of injury. As they get older, children can develop a better sense of what is safe to do and what helps them channel their energy, increasing their self-knowledge and sense of autonomy.

Helpful Modifications and Tools: If your child is being hyperactive inside the home in a way that is threatening their safety, enlist the child's help in outdoor activities that will channel their energy, such as gardening or washing the car. When the weather is warm, play a game of catch, go for a short hike, or take them swimming. In the winter, enlist their help in shoveling snow off a driveway or building a snowman.

INVESTIGATE BEHAVIORAL THERAPY

Targeted Challenges: Helps children with hyperactivity, inattention, and impulsivity. Increases adherence to a parent's or teacher's directions; prepares children for real-world consequences and increases a sense of personal autonomy.

Overview: To positively support and reinforce positive behavior in your child, consult with a trained behavioral therapist as an early step. Experts recommend that parents and teachers try behavioral therapy well before resorting to medication. Why? Although medication can certainly reduce symptoms like hyperactivity, inattention, and impulsivity, no medicine can actually change a child's behavior. In other words: Used in conjunction with behavioral therapy, medicine can help reduce a child's physiological symptoms.

It is essential—especially at an early age—to begin with any kind of therapy and assessment in managing your child's ADHD and helping them learn coping skills and a sense of autonomy. Usually, younger children respond well to behavioral therapy because their behaviors are relatively simple, and they do not yet have a great desire to separate themselves from their parents or challenge their rules and discipline. Start early if you can.

STRATEGY IMPLEMENTATION:

1. Practice positive reinforcement for behaviors you want to encourage in your child with the guidance of a skilled therapist.

2. Provide consistent consequences for negative behaviors.

3. Work on remaining consistent in your support and discipline with the help of a therapist.

4. Address your beliefs about parenting that may be interfering with implementing effective discipline for your child.

5. Though it can be difficult, share all your child's behaviors with your therapist, even those you'd rather not mention. The therapist can help you best if you are totally open and honest.

6. Make a long-term plan to consistently check in with the therapist, and be sure to update the plan as your child grows or as behaviors change.

7. Explore other physiological conditions that may mask themselves with ADHD symptoms.

Long-Term Considerations: Children who respond to this type of therapy show a decrease in negative behaviors over time and understand that these behaviors will be met with consistent consequences.

Helpful Modifications and Tools: If this type of therapy is not producing desired results, tweak your responses and consequences with the input of the therapist. Choose different responses, and see which ones are most effective at making your child more responsive to and engaged with the results of their actions. Keep a diary of your child's behaviors, and check in with the therapist consistently for feedback on both your child's development and your own.

INVESTIGATE MEDICATION

Targeted Challenges: Reduces the symptoms of inattention, hyperactivity, and impulsivity in children for whom it is recommended; gives children the ability to better understand their behaviors in conjunction with proper therapy; does not help children learn strategies for self-regulation.

Overview: Medication is not recommended as a first-line treatment for children under the age of six. The FDA requires that children be at least six to receive methylphenidate (Ritalin or Focalin, for example), though some doctors prescribe this type of medication off-label (meaning the medication is being used in a manner not specified in the FDA's approved packaging label) to children under six.

The largest study of preschoolers with ADHD, funded by the NIMH and published in 2006, studied about 300 preschoolers and their parents. The children started with a ten-week behavioral training course. The children who did not show improvement after the course of therapy were then given a low dose of methylphenidate or a placebo. The children who received medication showed a significant reduction in their symptoms compared to the group that received the placebo. However, almost one-third of the parents reported that the children who had received medication showed side effects of moderate to serious severity, including weight loss, loss of appetite, insomnia, anxiety, and emotional outburst. Eleven percent of the children in the study dropped out because their reactions to methylphenidate were so severe. In addition, after the study, the children who had received the medication were, on average, a half-inch and three pounds less than the mean of children who were not medicated.

STRATEGY IMPLEMENTATION:

1. Do not use medication as a first-line treatment for preschoolers with ADHD. Instead, try parent training techniques, modified classroom settings, and other strategies before considering medication for your child.

2. If you would like to investigate medication, consult a doctor who is experienced at working with children with ADHD and with any coexisting conditions your child may have.

3. Monitor long-term consequences and side effects of medication, and be sure to report them to your doctor so that the most effective medication can be prescribed.

Long-Term Considerations: If your child's symptoms cannot be controlled through behavioral strategies, parent training, or other strategies past the age of six, you can consider medication in conjunction with their doctor's advice. As your child ages, they may need different types of medication to respond to the changing needs of their developing minds and bodies. Be sure to check in regularly with your doctor and ask teachers and caregivers about your child's symptoms in other settings so that you are aware of how well the medication is working to control your child's symptoms.

 Helpful Modifications and Tools: Consult Russell A. Barkley's book, *Taking Charge of ADHD*, for more information about medication.

TRY YOGA FOR CHILDREN

Targeted Challenges: Helps children with hyperactivity, inattention, self-regulation, relaxation, and impulsivity.

Overview: Preschool-age children can benefit from alternative therapies, such as yoga and even simple meditation. Yoga can often help them relax to the point where they can close their eyes and concentrate on the intake and exhalation of their breath, allowing them to calm their bodies and minds. They may enjoy these activities outside or in a calming indoor place.

STRATEGY IMPLEMENTATION:

1. Use a yoga video or enroll your child in a yoga class. Choose videos and classes designed specifically for children. These classes are typically shorter in length.

2. Find a space where your child feels relaxed, such as a safe space indoors or a quiet place outside.

3. Allow your child to be active and stretch before they practice remaining still and calm.

Long-Term Considerations: Over time, children who practice yoga may find themselves more relaxed at all times of the day, even when they are not practicing yoga. They may also be less hyperactive and better able to attend to tasks.

Helpful Modifications and Tools: If your child is having difficulty practicing yoga indoors due to an inability to concentrate, have your child choose a spot outdoors where they feel comfortable. (Following your child's paths to comfort will encourage independence.) Your child may simply need to be part of a smaller class to avoid distractions or may do best practicing alone along with a yoga video.

REEVALUATE EDUCATIONAL SETTINGS AS YOUR CHILD GROWS

Targeted Challenges: Helps children maximize their academic potential and learn strategies to meet expected classroom behaviors.

Overview: When children are moving on to kindergarten, parents may need to assess which educational setting will be right for them. While preschool often builds movement and social training into the school day, many kindergartens offer largely sedentary routines and traditional, direct instruction. These types of settings may not be ideal for a child with ADHD and may worsen their symptoms, preventing them from advancing academically. It is imperative to find a school (or supportive staff within your current educational environment) that can help develop and affirm your child's strengths, skills, and learning style.

STRATEGY IMPLEMENTATION:

1. Seek help from a qualified professional if your child has a learning disability or speech issues. Many states provide early intervention services to help children whose speech or social skills are not developing in age-appropriate ways. Certified speech-language pathologists can help your child develop language skills. Getting help early is important for children who need these services. Without this type of intervention, a child can miss important milestones and development may be delayed.

2. Be sure that the professionals you choose are experienced at working with children who have similar issues, and that they are certified in their field (if their field recognizes certification).

Continued

3. Work with your local school district to understand the options open to your child in kindergarten. Some districts offer specialized settings with fewer children and more teachers or other staff in the classroom. Many districts will not provide this type of support until children have been formally diagnosed by a doctor or psychologist, so check what your district requires to provide your child with an IEP, if you feel that your child needs a specialized setting or other accommodations during the school day, such as breaks, or related services, such as speech-language therapy.

4. To implement an IEP, ask your child's school to evaluate your child in the areas of need. School personnel will then make a decision about the services or interventions your child requires. You can appeal if you do not agree with their decision. If an IEP is implemented, the school's team will meet regularly to review it and make modifications. Be sure to consult with your team about what you should ask for in your IEP meetings.

Long-Term Considerations: As children with ADHD grow older, they may require different types of settings. Some make an overall improvement in their functioning that makes additional support in school unnecessary. Other children exhibit coexisting learning disabilities as they get older, and they may need increased support. Parents need to evaluate their child's academic placement each academic year or if their child starts showing new academic, behavioral, or emotional needs. It is important that you become your child's fiercest advocate, because it is sadly very easy for children with ADHD to fall through the cracks in many school systems.

Here's a sample list of goals:

- **March:** Call my child's doctor for consultation about ADHD.

- **April:** Call the local ADHD group, such as Children and Adults with Attention Deficit/Hyperactivity Disorder (CHADD), about local parenting workshops; read a book about parenting children with ADHD and underline useful information.

- **May:** Begin to implement behavior plan; create safe space for my child to relax in nook in family room.

- **June:** Sign my child up for karate in a small class and make appointment with school board about plans for kindergarten.

- **July:** Reevaluate behavioral plan during summer months.

- **August:** Prepare for new school by setting up meeting with teachers.

This is one way to approach the steps you need to take to parent your preschooler. Try to set one or two realistic goals per month, and leave time to reevaluate whether your goals are working, and to adapt your plan if and when necessary.

Helpful Modifications and Tools: As you implement your parenting plan for your preschooler, keep in mind that change requires time. Make a chart of your goals and approach them over the span of several months to a year, and prepare for inevitable setbacks and times to reevaluate whether your approach is working. Build in goals that are realistic to achieve in the next few months, and use the resources available in your child's school and community.

School-Age Children

(AGES 6–12)

ADHD is commonly diagnosed for the first time among children of school-age children. This is because most mainstream schools require compliance to a rigid set of rules and the ability for children to complete tasks in a timely way, and it becomes obvious when a child with ADHD does not fit into that particular box. In addition, the criteria in the *DSM-5* for diagnosing ADHD mainly uses school-related behaviors (such as children getting out of their chairs or interrupting), though this diagnosis also requires that symptoms be present in another setting. There is no one-size-fits-all solution, and remember that ADHD can only be diagnosed by a trained professional.

Again, if your child has been diagnosed with ADHD at this age, it is imperative that you immediately consult with the school's special education department and begin the process of creating an IEP. You have had your child assessed by trained psychological professionals.

Do not let the school try to give your child a diagnosis or transfer them to an alternative school without an IEP. Unfortunately, in many communities, the accommodations and assistance recommended in the upcoming sections are not supported by the school system, and you may have to advocate for your child. As a parent you have many rights. The Resources section on page 148 has more information.

During these years, it's critical for you to help your child establish positive habits related to ADHD. For example, if their doctor prescribes medication, your child needs to understand that taking their medication is nonnegotiable. Many adolescents attempt to establish their independence by challenging their need to take medication. While children can be critical in helping their doctor understand how their medication is working, they need to understand that they are not in control of the decision whether or not to take medication that their doctor decides they need. In addition, children need to be educated about the dangers of sharing medications with their peers, as many adolescents are pressured to do so. If children understand these essential ground rules before adolescence, they will be in better shape when puberty hits. The school-age years are also critical for children to begin to establish good study habits and to understand how their mind works so that they can use their talents and navigate around roadblocks to achieve results in line with their academic potential.

The following are some strategies you can use for your school-age child to ensure you are advocating for the best care possible and providing a consistent parenting approach.

MOTIVATE THROUGH FEEDBACK AND PRAISE

Targeted Challenges: Helps children develop better self-regulation and adherence to discipline.

Overview: A school-age child with ADHD still requires a great deal of feedback, as they may still have issues with time, planning, and responding to consequences or discipline. Feedback about your child's behavior should be given regularly to get them on track, particularly during activities that require a great deal of sustained attention or that involve many detailed instructions. Research has shown that all kids, not just those with ADHD, respond better to praise when it is directed at their behavior—rather than at an overall assessment of their personality.

STRATEGY IMPLEMENTATION:

1. Provide praise that is fair and consistent, and that mention behavior rather than making a global assessment. For example, do not praise your child by saying, "You're such a great kid."

2. Comment on specific behaviors, even little ones. You could say things like, "I like the way you were so kind to your friend," or "You did a great job sitting still during the movie," or "I love what you made with your building set."

Long-Term Considerations: If children know you will praise their excellent behavior, they will also know that you will still love them if they don't always meet your standards. Let them know that your love and respect for them are unconditional, but that you will offer feedback on places to improve. Research conducted by experts like Carol Dweck, PhD, one of the world's leading researchers in the field of motivation, suggests that kids who hear their parents praise them, rather than their behaviors, are more afraid that they will lose their parents' love and esteem, so they become more fearful as a result.

ASK FOR SCHOOL ACCOMMODATIONS

Targeted Challenges: Helps children achieve their academic potential and work on coexisting learning disorders.

Overview: Children with ADHD may require specialized school placements starting in kindergarten or in later elementary grades. These accommodations can be granted as part of a 504 plan, which refers to section 504 of the Rehabilitation Act of 1973. This federal law prohibits discrimination based on a child's disability, and every school district in the country must abide by these regulations. These accommodations can also be covered by the Individuals with Disabilities Act (IDEA), which grants each child the right to a free appropriate public education that is designed to meet their needs and that prepares them for future employment, education, and independent living. Children with ADHD may require smaller classrooms with fewer distractions or preferential seating closer to the teachers so they can pay close attention—and so that the teacher can pay close attention to them as well. In addition, many schools have resource rooms with special education professionals as part of their programming. The close attention special ed teachers pay to an individual child's needs—in concert with proactive parenting and checking in with these teachers on a regular basis about your child's education plan—is invaluable.

STRATEGY IMPLEMENTATION:

1. Ask your child's school for appropriate accommodations in their school day, such as the ability to take breaks or extra time on tests. Children may need to get up and walk around during the school day, and your school should allow for this type of movement.

2. As your child gets older, ask for necessary accommodations on state-mandated or school-related tests, particularly if your child has coexisting learning disabilities.

3. Request a school-issued computer for typing assignments if your child has dysgraphia (a handwriting disorder) or other difficulty writing.

4. Ask your school for accommodations, such as the ability to listen to recordings of books as the child reads along. This does not mean that your child is not reading, but they may need to download audio files of books to listen and follow along. This process of listening and following along may help them develop into more fluent readers. However, they may also need the help of a reading specialist at school if they are falling behind their peers in their reading and writing development.

5. Have teachers provide your child with solutions to math problems in which some of the steps are already written down, so that your child only needs to solve some of the steps. Ask for graph paper, with plenty of space for the child to record answers.

Helpful Modifications and Tools: Over time, step back from helping your child complete homework assignments. Instead, help your child plan out their work on a nightly or weekly level, but resist doing the work for them. You may sit with them while they do the work for support, and coach them instead.

Special education programs typically place children in a resource room at school, with teachers and learning specialists who can help them develop strategies to complete their work. These types of professionals are trained and experienced at working with children with ADHD and with coexisting learning differences. If your school does not have a resource room or you receive resistance from the school, consider changing schools. Either way, it is essential to advocate for your child to have the resources they require to thrive.

In some cases, you may need to submit your child's formal diagnosis by a psychologist in order to continue to receive accommodations at school. As different diagnoses can possibly lead to different tracks in school, using an accurate diagnosis is critical to your child's future and the accommodations they will be able to access.

Having an IEP is a right, and you have the right to challenge any decision the school makes. If you are not happy with any aspect of your child's education, speak up. By advocating for your child, you can help them achieve their full potential. For more information about 504 plans and the IDEA, visit Wrightslaw.com. This site offers information about special education law and how to advocate for children with disabilities.

The process of finding a suitable educational setting for your child may be stressful, and possibly traumatic, for your child. Be supportive, but don't push. At appointments, let your child answer questions asked directly of them. Avoid speaking for them.

Avoid pathologizing your child. In other words, do not treat them as if they are abnormal or unhealthy. Also, make sure to listen to what they have to say. Sometimes, kids with ADHD, contrary to their behaviors in school, will simply shut down. Respect a child's need to process, and help them through it. As your child's parent and advocate, you have a great responsibility in guiding their educational program and sometimes their mental health.

DEVELOP CONSISTENT DISCIPLINE

Targeted Challenges: Helps children with hyperactivity, impulsivity, and difficulty following directions.

Overview: A child with ADHD may display behavioral and discipline problems as they grow older. While their peers are internalizing the demands of their teachers and parents, many children with ADHD internalize these demands at a much slower developmental rate, even if they understand them intellectually. Some of the behaviors of children with ADHD seem disobedient on purpose, but they often lack the cognitive development, self-control, and time management to be able to adhere to rules. However, they should always be held to manageable and realistic goals, and should be expected to work toward better discipline and listening skills.

STRATEGY IMPLEMENTATION:

1. Avoid yelling. While it may be tempting to simply yell at a child who is not listening, this type of response, while completely understandable (and inevitable at times), is not likely to be effective in the long term.

2. Tell your child in advance what is expected of them, and the consequences they will face if they do not behave.

3. Ask other caregivers to approach discipline in the same way so that your child is not getting mixed messages. Share your discipline systems with caregivers and other relatives, such as grandparents, so that everyone can be on the same page and approach your child in the same way.

4. Do not offer personalized criticism or overarching negative statements, such as "You'll never listen," or "Why can't you be like other kids?" Instead, after you've let your child know what is expected and made your expectations realistic, offer immediate consequences if the child does not follow directions. For example, tell your child they will get a time-out or will lose television time if they do not listen. Children with ADHD sometimes struggle to respond to far-away motivations or vague threats, so make the feedback concrete and immediate. That way, your child will begin to associate their behavior with the resulting consequences.

5. Try not to personalize your discipline. Connect it to their actions—not their personality. That way, the child will know the love you feel for them is separate from the idea that you do not accept poor behavior.

Long-Term Considerations: Children should begin to internalize what is required of them and should require less direction and discipline over time.

Helpful Modifications and Tools: If your discipline system is not working, tweak the consequences your child receives. Experiment with what approaches work best, and don't hesitate to compare notes with teachers and the special education department on their own methods of discipline with your child. Consult a behavioral therapist on methodologies and further strategies, especially if your plan of action doesn't seem to work.

KEEP TRACK OF TRIGGERS

Targeted Challenges: Helps children manage behavior and moods by recognizing what may trigger a shift.

Overview: Children with ADHD may have certain triggers in their environment that result in negative behaviors. If you understand your child's specific triggers, you may be able to modify their environment to reduce or eliminate some of their negative behaviors.

STRATEGY IMPLEMENTATION:

1. Observe what triggers your child's negative behaviors. Some common triggers for children with ADHD include:

    - Lack of sleep, worsening symptoms

    - Lack of exercise

    - A diet high in sugar or refined carbohydrates

    - Long periods of sedentary activities

    - Large crowds, either of other children or in public spaces

    - Too much homework that causes frustration

    - Too many demands given at the same time

    - Too much time playing video games or spending too much time online

2. Anticipate in advance what might set your child off, such as stressful times at school (exam weeks, major projects, etc.) and unstructured times such as long play dates, sleepovers, or family gatherings. Try to build relaxation into these periods. For example, if your child has a long research paper to write, work with them to set up a schedule in which they finish some of the

mini-steps involved in the project each day. Build relaxation, sleep, and exercise into the schedule. If your child is resistant to getting started, have them work with a teacher, resource room teacher, or tutor so that they can do a bit of work on the project over time and avoid feeling overly stressed or anxious.

Long-Term Considerations: By keeping track of what sets your child off, you will get a sense of what triggers your child to act in negative ways. You can start by trying to modify your child's environment to remove elements such as too much screen time, and, over time, children should start understanding what's difficult for them and develop strategies to handle or eliminate these issues. This type of self-awareness might take time, but it's critical to developing strategies that your child will continue to use into adolescence and adulthood.

Helpful Modifications and Tools: At the same time you are noting what provokes your child to act negatively, keep track of what precedes positive behavior, such as activity, sufficient sleep, exercise, listening to music, dancing, and other activities, so you can build these antecedents to positive behavior into their schedule.

Use Worksheet #2 to keep track of the preexisting conditions or antecedents of your child's behaviors. This will help you better understand what sets off their negative behaviors. For each negative behavior, try to note what came before (the "A" or antecedent, the "B" or behavior, and the "C" or consequence).

WORKSHEET #2: ABCs of Behavior

When tracking the activities that precede your child's behavior, note any extenuating circumstances that you think might be exacerbating your child's reactions. Rate your child's behavior on a scale of 1 to 10, with 1 indicating very negative behavior and 10 indicating very positive behavior.

ANTECEDENT (WHAT HAPPENED BEFORE THE BEHAVIOR)		CHILD'S MOOD OR BEHAVIOR	BEHAVIOR RATING	CONSEQUENCE (WHAT HAPPENED AS A RESULT)
TRIGGER	EXTENUATING CONSEQUENCES?			
Doing homework	Rainy day today so no soccer practice	Fidgety, whiny, bored	8	Homework took twice as long to do; needed extra coaxing

DEVELOP TIME-MANAGEMENT SKILLS

Targeted Challenges: Helps children with time management, planning, and execution of their work.

Overview: By third or fourth grade, your child will expected to complete tasks independently. Though these tasks are usually short and simple, it is important that kids start working on them independently, if they can. However, children with ADHD tend to not have an innate sense of time and may have difficulty planning. It's your job to help them build and reinforce these skills.

STRATEGY IMPLEMENTATION:

1. Work with your child to create a realistic schedule. For example, if they are assigned a report that's due in a week, you can help them create a schedule in which they take notes on their topic for two days, write an outline one day, write a rough draft one day, and revise and finish their paper another day.

2. Encourage your child to begin completing their homework on their own, building the independence and skills they will need for middle school and high school. Again, a child may need the extra moral support of a parent, and while it is more than all right to suggest to a child that you will sit with them and coach them, don't do their homework for them.

3. Show your child the way you conduct your daily life, as an example of just one learning style. If there are other adults in your home, have them do the same. Talk openly about the challenges you faced when you were their age and how you

Continued

overcame them. Even if your child doesn't work on tasks the way you do, seeing the patterns that you and other adults have will help them recognize that everyone has different ways of conducting their own lives and that their unique qualities may call for them to come up with their own solutions. This enables them to further develop a sense of autonomy.

4. Build in external reminders of time into your child's schedule. For example, set a timer for twenty or thirty minutes at the start of each task. When the timer goes off, it will indicate that it's time to move on. It will further serve to develop and reinforce the child's internal sense of the passage of time.

Long-Term Considerations: Over time, using external reminders and a schedule can help children develop a more realistic sense of what this period of time feels like. Through this process, they can develop skills to complete their work more efficiently and plan ahead for assignments.

Helpful Modifications and Tools: If your child is still struggling with the ability to plan, organize their work, and shift from one task to another (sometimes called executive function skills), they may need extra resources such as a learning specialist at school or private instruction at home. Sometimes, children respond to an adult who is not their parent: tutors or other adult figures can sometimes break through where parents cannot.

Use Worksheet #3 to help your child start keeping a homework log. This list covers a lot of ground, including the project's due date, start and finish times, and a section to note what helped or hindered completion of their work.

WORKSHEET #3: Homework Tracker

When tracking homework, experiment with different ways of breaking down homework assignments into smaller tasks, and keep an eye on circumstances that seem to facilitate efficient homework completion or hinder it. Use this information to generate a list of helpful tips in the lines below.

HOMEWORK		START DATE	DUE DATE	CIRCUMSTANCES	
ASSIGNMENT	ASSIGNMENT TASKS			WHAT HELPED	WHAT HINDERED
Math Test	Create math study sheet	Sun 10/4	Mon 10/5	Working in den while parents read	Lost math book for a while; was found under the bed
	Study sheet every day	Mon 10/5	Fri 10/9	Reviewing @ same time daily before TV time	Lost study sheet, found crumpled @ bottom of book bag

Based on the above information, it seems that the following tips may be helpful:

- Get in habit of keeping school books on the study table in the den
- Keep study sheet in clear plastic folder (the one w/ math stickers on it)
- _____
- _____
- _____

GETTING STARTED ON TASKS

Targeted Challenges: Helps children initiate and plan tasks.

Overview: Children with ADHD may find it very difficult to start a project, task, or activity. It's also sometimes difficult for them to end one mental or physical activity and then shift right over to the next. This can be one of the hardest things for children with ADHD to achieve. School-age children with ADHD often need an adult to help them plan and get started. Keep in mind that there are cognitive reasons that can make these tasks difficult. While their behavior may cause you frustration, remember that your child is not always being purposefully difficult (though any child can certainly develop resistance and poor coping skills). Be as supportive as you can while helping your child develop initiation and planning skills.

STRATEGY IMPLEMENTATION:

1. Notice what makes it easier for your child to make transitions and get started on a new task.

2. Provide your child with a short break between tasks; a longer break might make it too hard for them to get started on what they need to do next.

3. Provide the ability for them to move around during their break, but encourage your child to avoid television, video games, or online activities. These activities might distract them too much.

4. Experiment to help your child discover what they can do during breaks to recharge in body and mind, so they can start on the next task. For instance, some kids love being in the kitchen; find some simple baking recipes for which the prep will fill a fifteen-minute break, and the cooking time will coincide with their next break. This schedule also teaches multitasking.

5. Alternatively, if your child tends toward hyperactivity, your child may need to exercise or let out all of the energy they store up from sitting still. Let them run around the yard, shoot hoops, or jump rope for the allotted time. Or they may wish to sit quietly and play imaginative games. Every child is different; follow your child's lead and structure breaks around their particular needs.

6. Set a timer to make sure their break does not go on for too long.

Long-Term Considerations: Over time, children should develop ways to motivate themselves to initiate tasks. With good support and feedback—and firm but kind reinforcement of the rules of task time—it is very possible to help your child develop an innate ability to get started and stay on task.

Helpful Modifications and Tools: If your child is still struggling with task initiation after trying to incorporate short breaks into their schedules, investigate another form of help, such as cognitive behavioral therapy (CBT) and/or medication.

INVESTIGATE COGNITIVE BEHAVIORAL THERAPY

Targeted Challenges: Helps children with inattention, impulsivity, and hyperactivity, and also helps their parents reinforce positive behaviors.

Overview: Children who have sufficient verbal skills can benefit from cognitive behavioral therapy (CBT). This is a specific type of psychological approach in which parents learn how to increase positive behaviors and reduce negative behaviors associated with the core ADHD symptoms of inattention, hyperactivity, and impulsivity, and helps children develop better ways to regulate themselves. This type of therapy can help children with impulsive behavior, who often have difficulty interacting with their parents because they are prone to tantrums and to not listening to directions.

STRATEGY IMPLEMENTATION:

1. Find a therapist who is trained in CBT. Many therapists say they address ADHD symptoms and behaviors in children, but they may not be trained in CBT. The Association for Behavioral and Cognitive Therapies (see the Resources section on page 150) maintains a list of trained therapists on their website. When interviewing potential therapists, verify that the therapist has specific experience implementing strategies that help children with ADHD and their families.

2. Attend parent training for about twelve sessions, which helps you learn to reinforce desired behaviors and reduce unwanted behaviors in your child through using praise and rewards. For example, if your child pays attention or responds to your requests, you will learn how to praise or reward them in ways that reinforce their good behavior.

3. Interact with your child while, in some cases, the therapist observes behind a one-way mirror and communicates with you via an earpiece.

4. Listen and respond to the therapist's instruction about how to provide positive feedback and use swift consequences, such as time-outs, for negative behavior.

5. Reinforce new parenting skills with parental homework between sessions.

6. Keep in mind that the goal of this type of therapy isn't to get rid of ADHD. Instead, it's to provide your child with strategies that will ease their functioning in school, at home, and in the wider world.

Long-Term Considerations: Because they are provided with positive reinforcement and know what consequences they can expect, children often show dramatic improvement in their behavior, and parents reinforce their own skills with practice homework between sessions. Most CBT interventions are designed to last about twelve weeks or twelve sessions, but many families decide to attend sessions for longer periods.

> **Helpful Modifications and Tools:** Talk to your child's teacher about creating a daily report card, in which they note positive behaviors your child exhibits with stars—for example, finishing work, waiting their turn, and staying in their seat. If your child has enough stars, they can get a reward at home such as time playing video games or at school by spending time with the school's pet or a few extra minutes at recess.

INVESTIGATE MEDICATION

Targeted Challenges: Helps reduce symptoms of inattention, hyperactivity, and impulsivity in children in conjunction with therapy.

Overview: If your child does not respond to parent training and behavioral training, you may wish to consult with a prescribing physician (who might be a psychiatrist, neurologist, or pharmacologist) about medication. Stimulant therapy as well as other types of ADHD medication is indicated (and often recommended) for children with ADHD who are over age seven. While taking this medication does not cure ADHD, it can help reduce the symptoms of inattention and impulsivity to the point at which the child can better learn strategies. Experts generally suggest that the combination of medication and learning strategies is optimal for helping these children develop.

STRATEGY IMPLEMENTATION:

1. Realize that it is never an easy decision to decide whether or not ADHD medication is right for your child, but there is no doubt that some children (and adults) thrive on ADHD medication.

2. When working with a prescribing physician, be sure to schedule regular checkups. It is imperative that your child is regularly monitored.

3. Observe your child's behaviors and symptoms over time, and report back to your doctor about these symptoms, any side effects you are seeing in your child, and any feedback your child gives you.

4. Consult the section in chapter 4 on Managing Common Side Effects from Medication on page 47 to find out more information about how to handle side effects that may develop.

Helpful Modifications and Tools: Keep in mind that it can take some time for your child's dose to reach its maximum efficacy, and that it is not uncommon to have a difficult time finding the right dose at first. In other words, don't fret if the medication doesn't have an immediate effect. Your child is adjusting to the medication. Ask your child if they'd like to keep a diary about how they feel as the medication regimen begins.

Share information about your child's medication with their teachers. The school nurse will have to be informed as well, even if your child does not receive medication in school. Some children require a boost in the middle of the day or before doing homework at night.

Monitor your child's symptoms carefully. Ask for the input and observations of teachers and caregivers, as well as your child, so your doctor can provide the most effective type and dose of medication to your child.

Educate your child about the dangers of sharing medication with peers, who may be particularly interested in taking stimulant medication. Remind your child that it is illegal and perilous to share medication. Many adolescents falsely believe that taking ADHD medications will improve their performance, but this is a myth that your child should know about.

Remind your child that taking medication is not open to discussion if a doctor has recommended it. While children can be very helpful in letting their parents and doctors know how the medication is making them feel and they can contribute to the discussion about which medications to take, they are not yet equipped to decide on their own whether or not to take the medication.

CREATE AN ADHD-FRIENDLY HOME

Targeted Challenges: Helps reduce hyperactivity and the risk of injury in the home.

Overview: No matter which modifications are made at school, some children with ADHD do not find that school caters to their interests and talents, and feel profoundly uncomfortable there. Home should be a safe haven, a place where they feel comfortable and able to express themselves. However, as with preschoolers, school-age children with ADHD may also require modifications to their physical environment. Homes might have to be safety-proofed, as children with hyperactivity in particular are prone to injuring themselves.

STRATEGY IMPLEMENTATION:

1. Design a room with your child that feels comfortable and welcoming to them. Let them pick the colors and themes, and fill the room with the types of toys and games they love the most. Make it a special space that channels their unique energy, and includes various modes of relaxing elements, such as a NERF-style basketball hoop, pillows, and music. While your child might want a television or video game console in the room, these are not ideal for a child who needs greater reinforcement to read, complete tasks, or socialize in productive ways with others.

2. If your child tends toward impulsivity or has destructive tendencies, make modifications in your home that involve moving valuable or breakable objects to a safe place.

3. Because children with hyperactivity can be a little accident-prone, you'll want to choose durable, sturdy furnishings for your home. Large bookcases and heavy items should be secured to the wall or floor, and they should be made of materials that are easier to keep clean.

4. Use wall organizers, calendars, bulletin boards, and charts to display notes, reminders, and other signs. Place them in areas of the house where your child can see them easily, and use them to help your child develop their organizational skills.

5. Designate special areas where important items, like house keys and lunch boxes, are always kept. Many children with ADHD find it easier to keep track of their belongings if they develop a habit of keeping their belongings in the same places.

Helpful Modifications and Tools: Children with ADHD often have sleep issues, especially when experimenting with medication. Using electronic devices close to bedtime can disrupt their sleep–wake cycle and make sleeping difficult.

Do not charge electronic devices in your child's rooms, as the light emitted from these devices can keep them awake.

Review the Resources section on page 148 to find software and applications that help children with ADHD at home. For instance, White Noise, an app available on iTunes, allows your child to choose different types of white noises to help them sleep.

UNDERSTAND AND HELP YOUR DAUGHTER WITH ADHD

Targeted Challenges: Helps girls with ADHD improve their self-confidence.

Overview: Girls with ADHD face particular challenges. According to the Centers for Disease Control and Prevention (CDC), girls are diagnosed less often than boys with ADHD; this is because many girls often manifest with the inattentive forms of ADHD than with the more hyperactive-impulsive symptoms of the condition. However, they still struggle and often underachieve in school, and they may be more likely than boys to blame themselves for, and internalize, their problems. As a result, girls with ADHD often develop an acute sense of their personal failures—and they may not even realize that they have ADHD. As they approach adolescence, they struggle with the behavior of girls around them, and they are expected to understand a myriad of oft-outdated social mores and pressures that sadly persist today. These complicated social "rules" can be confounding for anyone, and they can be very hard for girls with ADHD to decipher.

STRATEGY IMPLEMENTATION:

1. Connect your daughter with a local ADHD support group, particularly one expressly for girls. Often, if they receive help in a resource room or special education program at school, they may be in the minority, surrounded by boys who may or may not share their exact needs or their presentation of ADHD. They may also feel stigmatized by being one of a few girls with ADHD who is grouped with boys.

2. Read *Women with Attention Deficit Disorder* by Sari Solden. This is an informative and supportive resource to help parents and children understand the unique challenges ADHD has

for women of all ages, and it contains many suggestions to overcome them. Consult this book often, and share it with your daughter when she gets older. Read other books on the topic, such as *Understanding Girls with AD/HD* by Kathleen Nadeau, Ellen Littman, and Patricia O. Quinn.

3. Connect your daughter with a peer group of like-minded girls. If your daughter feels that she cannot find a supportive group of friends at school, see how she feels about attending community youth groups in the community, such as 4-H, the Girl Scouts, or a private athletic academy. Martial arts programs can be very helpful, and often have programs specifically for girls and women.

Long-Term Considerations: If your daughter operates outside societal norms, help her find her own set of values, personalities, and strengths. Remain positive about her expression and behavior and affirm it. It is also very helpful for your daughter to be introduced to role models who have lived their lives outside the box of what society "expects" of women.

 Helpful Modifications and Tools: In the Resources section on page 148, you will find additional titles that can help you and your daughter learn more about the way ADHD presents itself in girls and women.

DEMYSTIFY ADHD AS YOUR CHILD GROWS

Targeted Challenges: Helps children understand ADHD, improves their understanding of themselves, and increases their self-confidence.

Overview: *While it may be hard for a very young child to understand what ADHD is and how it affects them, as children grow, they can learn more about what ADHD means. Sadly, many parents resist telling their children that they have ADHD, but children will almost always sense that they are different from their peers in some way. In addition, children with ADHD usually receive constant feedback that they are not following directions or living up to what is expected of them—from parents (often unwittingly), teachers, and others. If they don't understand that they have ADHD, they may simply feel that they are lacking in some way and cannot match up.*

STRATEGY IMPLEMENTATION:

1. Introduce your child to the idea of ADHD simply at first, either through you or through a trusted doctor or therapist.

2. Explain that ADHD is a condition they were born with and that their difficulties are not their fault.

3. Help them understand how these difficulties affect them, and that those difficulties can be overcome if your child can develop strategies or methods to help themselves.

4. To learn more, seek books targeted toward parents with younger children, such as Kathy Hoopmann's charming book, *All Dogs Have ADHD*. This book uses adorable pictures of dogs to help children understand the core symptoms of ADHD in a positive, encouraging fashion. This fun and humorous book helps children of this age view ADHD in a way that celebrates being "different."

5. As they get older, introduce your child to more sophisticated books about ADHD. Discuss how it might affect them, as well as the help and strategies available to them.

6. Children with ADHD don't always recognize their strengths, and usually these strengths are not pointed out to them or rewarded. It is your job as a parent to recognize and encourage your child's unique abilities, and to broadcast that to your child's support network at school or any other activity. Why is this so important at a young age? There are many adults with ADHD who have been very successful in their chosen fields, but who still feel like failures because many of them grew up with undiagnosed ADHD. They received so much negative feedback growing up that they never came to understand or appreciate their own merits. As a result, they were not able, even as adults, to understand and embrace their very real strengths, even if they were ultimately successful.

Long-Term Considerations: Children who know they have ADHD may understand that they face challenges, but it is important to affirm that these challenges do not mean that are bad people or less smart than their peers. Instead, they have to embrace the fact that in some cases they have to work harder than other people at tasks that may seem effortless for others. At the same time, recognizing their own strengths—and having those strengths celebrated—can help them overcome some of those obstacles.

Teenagers
(AGES 13–19)

Adolescence can be a difficult time for children and parents, but it can be particularly hard for teenagers with ADHD. Increased demands at school may mean they are unable to manage what is required of them, while the desire to be independent leads them to reject assistance from parents and teachers who want to help them get a handle on it.

With the large amount of schoolwork in middle school and high school, students are required to pay constant attention in class and are expected to complete a great deal of homework. As a result, teens with ADHD may find themselves unable to keep up with the academic demands. They may also have the contradictory and confusing experience of knowing they are smart but feeling as if they do not measure up to their classmates.

In addition, teenagers with ADHD may show poor judgment and impulsivity; they may place themselves in dangerous situations that involve drinking, driving, and being around others who might not treat them well, for instance. It's critical for them to understand how to judge whether their peers are true friends. Their judgment may make them prone to making hasty or ill-considered decisions about discontinuing their medication or therapies, even if they need them, rather than working with their parents and other professionals to find medication and therapies that work for them and that make them feel comfortable. Finally, they can also be pressured into sharing their medication with their friends or acquaintances—which is dangerous and against the law.

If teenagers are made aware of some of these temptations and obstacles in advance, they may avoid them. Because teens often don't listen to their parents, they should arrive at adolescence with a good understanding of how to ask for help, how to evaluate who their true friends are, and how to respect the line at which their independence and freedom end (for example, in choosing whether to take their medication). Armed with knowledge and strategies, they can thrive even during the rocky years of adolescence by finding out more about who they are, what they love to do, and what their future will hold.

Here are some strategies you can use to help your teen manage their symptoms and go on to achieve success.

CREATE A BEHAVIORAL CONTRACT

Targeted Challenges: Helps teenagers with impulsivity and negative behaviors.

Overview: Adolescents with ADHD may still not have internalized what is required of them to succeed in their endeavors, and they may show increasing resistance to following their parents' demands. As a result, it's easy to get into constant battles with them. It is important to develop strategies to avoid arguments while reinforcing discipline.

STRATEGY IMPLEMENTATION:

1. Working with your child, your child's other parent (if present) or your partner, and possibly an outside therapist or other adult your child respects, make a contract that specifies the important behaviors you expect from your child.

2. Include only those behaviors that are critical, such as cleaning up their room, doing their homework, and obeying curfews. Remember that teens will be annoyed by almost everything you ask, even if it's reasonable, so concentrate on the behaviors that are critical to keep them functioning in school and at home and to keep them safe.

3. Spell out with great specificity in writing what is required of your child, and what the consequences are if the rules are not followed. Write all these rules down and put them in a place where everyone can see them.

4. Have your child sign the contract so that their agreement is clearly made. Respond to infractions by immediately giving your child the consequences spelled out in the contract.

5. Try to avoid arguing with your child. Instead, give a gentle reminder of the child's role in keeping up the contract.

Long-Term Considerations: Over time, your child should learn what the consequences of breaking one part of the contract would be. For example, if your daughter does not finish her project that was due Friday, the hard consequence is that she must not go out on Saturday night. Don't let it slide if it happens. It may be painful for both of you, but there need to be hard lines drawn in these types of situations. However, there is a line between discipline and abuse. Don't limit your teen from important community events and social gatherings, as they are also important to development. Sometimes, you must bend your own rules—but make it the rare exception, and only for the sake of the child.

Helpful Modifications and Tools: If your child does not follow these rules despite the consequences, you must revise the consequences. You may also have to consult with a professional, such as a therapist or guidance counselor, if your child is consistently not living up to expectations. Work with your team to best support your child. Again, a plan and goals should be spelled out on the IEP.

Keep in mind that as children begin adolescence, signs of other coexisting conditions (such as depression, anxiety, bipolar disorder, gender dysphoria, and eating disorders) may begin presenting alongside ADHD. It is imperative to continue to evaluate your child, as ADHD symptoms mask many of these conditions.

Make sure your medical and psychological team is composed of the best professionals you can find and that your child is comfortable with each one. If your child is uncomfortable with any doctor or other medical professional on the team, listen to them, and try to solve the problem—don't force your child to attend a session they are not comfortable with. Give your teen the opportunity to make decisions about their medical care. Though teens can be rebellious, when they are treated with respect and empathy, and have the power to make some of their own decisions, they can show incredible maturity and self-awareness.

Use Worksheet #4 as a sample template for the contract you construct with your teenager.

WORKSHEET #4: **Behavioral Contract**

Alex is a fifteen-year-old sophomore in high school who worked out this contract with his parents

I, _____*Alex*_____ , promise to take care of the following daily responsibilities:

1. *finish homework & show it to my parents by 9 p.m. every night*
2. *set the table for dinner at 6:30 p.m*
3. *pack my backpack for the next day by 9:30 p.m*

When I complete my responsibilities, I will be allowed the following daily rewards:

On school nights, my parents will allow me to spend 30 minutes on Facebook. On weekends, I get to spend 1 hour on Facebook

I will not be allowed these rewards if I fail to meet my responsibilities. If I go beyond the limits of my reward, I may suffer the following consequences:

My Facebook privileges may be revoked. If I spend more than my allotted time on Facebook, then my parents will install a time management application like Rescue Time on my laptop to make sure the site is blocked after the allotted time has passed for the day

This contract will be reviewed on _____*the last day of school*_____ .

DISCUSS MEDICATION AND MEDICATION ABUSE

Targeted Challenges: Helps teenagers manage their medication in safe ways, particularly if they are impulsive or have poor decision-making abilities.

Overview: Teenagers with ADHD may require stimulant medication into high school and college, and they may also require additional medication for coexisting conditions, such as anxiety and depression. Unfortunately, many of their peers may abuse substances, and may ask your child to sell them or give them pills in the mistaken belief that the medication will help them improve their grades or performance in school or sports. Research has shown that medication for ADHD does not help people who don't have ADHD, but this rumor persists. The abuse of stimulant medication has become rampant, with teenagers without ADHD more likely to abuse other drugs and alcohol than teenagers with ADHD who are prescribed the right doses of medication.

STRATEGY IMPLEMENTATION:

1. Have an honest conversation with your child about the dangers of taking medication that is not prescribed to them. Let them know that sharing ADHD medication is illegal, unethical, and can possibly cause their friends and other peers great harm.

Long-Term Considerations: Teenagers will become responsible for handling their own medication in college. They need to understand whether they should take the medication on a daily basis or take it as needed, such as before a big exam. Eventually, they need to understand how the medication affects them physiologically, their own physiological symptoms of ADHD, and how to manage symptoms with or without medication. They also need both the confidence and capacity to begin managing their own health care without parental supervision.

DEVELOP TIME-MANAGEMENT AND PLANNING SKILLS

Targeted Challenges: Helps teenagers with executive function skills, such as time management, planning, and organization.

Overview: Teenagers with ADHD may continue to struggle with planning, organization, task initiation, and completion (executive function skills). There is some evidence that many children with ADHD may take longer to fully develop their executive function skills than previously thought. For some people, this brain development continues well into their twenties. However, their schoolwork and possibly their job may present them with large demands on their executive functioning, so parents or teachers can help teenagers develop necessary planning and organizational skills.

STRATEGY IMPLEMENTATION:

1. Teach your teen to use a planner or calendar to break down longer assignments into daily smaller tasks, and have them backdate an assignment from the due date. Before a large assignment is due, they should have several smaller steps laid out in their calendars. They may need explicit help from a parent or teacher in understanding how to space out a larger assignment.

2. If they do not complete one step in the process, let them know that they can move it to the next day and do not have to fear they will fail entirely to complete the larger task.

3. Use a sheet to help them record when they started and stopped each homework assignment and what hindered or helped them complete the assignment.

4. If they are struggling with motivation, have them reward themselves with a break or an activity they like for completing one step of the process.

Long-Term Considerations: Over time, teenagers should develop a more realistic sense of how to plan longer-term assignments and how to stay motivated to complete each step of a process.

Helpful Modifications and Tools: If your child is struggling to complete these types of longer assignments or is offering a lot of resistance, enlist the help of a learning specialist, a professional who has training (in a field such as special education or psychology) and experience helping children with ADHD.

If your child is spending too much time on computers or the Internet, use an application such as RescueTime (see the Resources section on page 148). This program helps people track their computer and Internet use, set goals, and monitor their progress. In addition, some versions of the program allow users to block sites if they have already been on them for the allotted time for that day. For example, if users agree to spend 30 minutes on Twitter, the program will block their access to that site after 30 minutes have passed for that day.

Consult with your child's doctor if your child is on medication but is still not able to complete homework. The doctor may need to adjust their dose. Follow up with the doctor about any side effects you see. For example, some children who take ADHD medication close to bedtime may suffer from insomnia.

Use Worksheet #5 to help your child track their homework assignments. Also, the applications and programs listed in the Resource section on page 148 provide help for those who struggle with distraction or disorganization.

WORKSHEET #5: Homework Tracker

When tracking homework, experiment with different ways of breaking down homework assignments into smaller tasks, and keep an eye on circumstances that seem to facilitate efficient homework completion or hinder it. Because teens have such a high workload, they may need additional tools, such as productivity apps, to help them. Use this information to generate a list of helpful tips in the lines below.

| HOMEWORK | | START DATE | DUE DATE | CIRCUMSTANCES | |
ASSIGNMENT	ASSIGNMENT TASKS			WHAT HELPED	WHAT HINDERED
3-page English paper	Read the book	Sun 10/4	Sun 10/11	Family reading time after dinner	Reading on iPad too many tempting apps on there
	Brainstorm ideas	Mon 10/12	Wed 10/14		
	Create outline	Thu 10/15	Mon 10/19		
	Write rough draft	Tue 10/20	Fri 10/23		
	Revise and finish!	Sat 10/24	Wed 10/28		

Based on the above information, it seems that the following tips may be helpful:

- Try better parental controls on iPad, Dad's old Kindle, or paper books
-
-

IMPROVE STUDY SKILLS

Targeted Challenges: Helps teenagers whose inattention or problems with working memory interfere with schoolwork or who have coexisting learning disorders.

Overview: Many adolescents with ADHD are very bright; however, they often underachieve in school due to inattention, hyperactivity, and poor working memory. They also may have coexisting learning disabilities.

STRATEGY IMPLEMENTATION:

1. Discover strategies and accommodations that work. For instance, to help a child memorize information and work around a poor working memory (which is the ability to hold information in mind for a short period and use it until the information is transferred to long-term memory), have them chunk or combine information using mnemonic devices. These are types of memory aids, such as using the first letter of each word in a list of information to spell out another word. For example, instead of memorizing that Turkey, Austria, and Germany were on one side during World War I, your child can use the abbreviation "TAG." This abbreviation will make the information easier to remember and reduce the overall memory demand, as memorizing "TAG" is easier than memorizing "Turkey, Austria, and Germany."

2. If your child struggles with reading because of inattention or a coexisting reading or language challenge such as dyslexia, encourage them to read along while listening to an audiobook. This strategy will help improve comprehension and fluency, and will help your child keep up with the reading demands in middle school and high school.

Continued

3. Consider whether your child needs special accommodations for standardized or state tests. Be sure to speak with the guidance counselor or learning specialist at your school about how to apply for these types of accommodations and the type of documentation you will need far in advance of the test day.

Long-Term Considerations: Over time, your child may understand how to use preferred methods to study. For example, if your child is an auditory learner who understands information presented aloud, they can listen to the information or say it aloud before a test. They will also learn to space out studying over time to avoid cramming everything into the last minute.

Helpful Modifications and Tools: If your child is still struggling to learn information and prepare for tests, enlist the help of a teacher, learning specialist, or another professional. Speak to the guidance or counseling staff at your school to find out what's available in-house, or ask for a referral to a professional.

BE A STUDY DOUBLE

Targeted Challenges: Helps teenagers with distractibility or difficulty initiating tasks.

Overview: Many people with ADHD find that they can start tasks and attend to them better when they are sitting with another person.

STRATEGY IMPLEMENTATION:

1. To be a study double, sit at the table with your child when they begin their work. Do not interfere with your child's work or how they begin the work.

2. Model good behavior, such as persisting in a sedentary task, by doing your own work or reading with them.

3. Model good habits, such as taking refreshing breaks without getting distracted and failing to return to work, so that your child can learn how to develop those habits, too.

Long-Term Considerations: Over time, your child may not need this type of support, but it can help them get started. Once started, your child may realize they can finish the task on their own.

Helpful Modifications and Tools: If you find this strategy is not working, your child may need a nonparental study double; ask them if they would like to invite a peer or another family member to study with them. Sometimes, it can be hard for teens to work with their parents, but they may be able to work with another person.

DEMYSTIFY ADHD AND DISCUSS ITS CHANGING NATURE

Targeted Challenges: Helps teenagers improve their understanding of themselves and boost their self-confidence and self-awareness.

Overview: As children get older, they are ready to understand more information about what ADHD is and how their mind works. You can help them understand what ADHD is and how it affects them, and how they can use ADHD's unique pluses, such as a great ability for multitasking, to enhance their life and education.

STRATEGY IMPLEMENTATION:

1. Help your child learn about ADHD in different ways. Some children respond well to speaking with their doctor, psychologist, or other therapist. Others will respond to speaking with a family friend or an adult they trust who also has ADHD.

2. Provide your teen with books about ADHD. Start older teens with *Driven to Distraction* by Edward Hallowell and John Ratey. This classic was recently updated and contains many stories about people with ADHD, an explanation of what the disorder is and how it presents itself, and tips on how to manage it. The authors also present the positive side of ADHD and the benefits it confers, including high energy, innovation, and creativity. The book is easily readable and is available as an audiobook.

3. As teens read these books and speak about ADHD with professionals and caregivers, they may want to make a list of what does and does not apply to them. For example, on a piece of paper, they can write down areas in which they are thriving, such as sports and social relationships. They can then write down areas that they are working on and making headway in, such as finishing long-term assignments, paying attention in class, and controlling their anger. Finally, they can write down

areas in which they feel they need to improve, such as listening to parents and teachers. For each area, they can identify whether their successes or challenges arise in part from having ADHD. In this way, they can understand how having ADHD may affect, but not control, their behavior and how having ADHD has also helped them in certain ways.

4. If your child feels comfortable doing so, they can volunteer to work with younger children with ADHD or other issues. This type of work helps older kids understand how far they've come and helps them develop patience and understanding of themselves and others. It can also help them feel a lot more confident and compassionate.

Long-Term Considerations: Over time, adolescents should develop not only an awareness of their own form of ADHD, but also a better awareness of how they learn and function productively. Many people with ADHD and/or learning differences are better than others at understanding their needs, how their own minds work, and themselves because they have had to develop this sense to manage their ADHD.

Helpful Modifications and Tools: If your child is not ready to hear about ADHD or learn more about how it affects them, don't despair. Instead, try revisiting the subject after they have matured a bit more. Also, keep in mind that it may be difficult for a child to take in this information when they are feeling down. It might be easier to digest after a success at school, in a concert, in a play, or on the athletic field. The Resources section on page 148 includes a list of books, magazines, and websites that can help teenagers learn more about ADHD.

ADHD COACHING

Targeted Challenges: Helps teenagers learn how to develop customized strategies to manage ADHD and achieve success.

Overview: ADHD coaches come from different fields. Some are trained as social workers or psychologists, while others come from freestanding coaching academies that are not usually associated with universities. Some coaches are people who have ADHD. Coaches work with teenagers, as well as adults, to help them develop practical strategies to manage their ADHD symptoms.

STRATEGY IMPLEMENTATION:

1. Ask your school or doctor for a referral to an experienced ADHD coach. Keep in mind that ADHD coaching is not intended to replace psychotherapy or work with a trained mental health professional or a medical doctor.

2. Interview a potential coach for fifteen to thirty minutes. When speaking to the coach, find out more about their methods, fees, and structure. Make sure that the coach has worked with teenagers with ADHD who faced the same issues as your child. Some coaches work with people over the phone, while others meet with people in person. Ask what the coach generally focuses on, e.g., time management, paper management, and/or organization of daily tasks.

3. Have your child work with the coach to formulate goals. Though some of the goals can come from you, it's helpful for your teenager to develop their own goals. This step will increase buy-in and motivation, and your teen will also improve their self-knowledge and self-awareness.

4. Some common goals for ADHD coaching for teens might include developing a better sense of time, developing more independence in daily life, or learning how to manage one's work and time efficiently. The coach will work with your child to develop and implement strategies to help them move toward their goals. Of course, the ultimate responsibility for achieving the goals is in your child's hands. While the coach can suggest strategies that have worked for others, only your child can put these strategies into place and keep using them over time.

5. Make sure the goals you and your child set with the coach are realistic and achievable within about three months. Many coaching clients tend to drop out after about five weeks if they don't see progress, but try to have your child stick with coaching for a bit longer if you feel like the coach is offering sound strategies.

Long-Term Considerations: Over time, your child should start to internalize the strategies and tips the coach offers, and incorporate them into their daily routine. In addition, you should start to see progress in the areas you and your child have targeted, such as increased efficiency in homework, a less cluttered desk, and an adherence to the rules of the house.

Helpful Modifications and Tools: If coaching does not work, your child might need to work with a cognitive behavioral therapist or another professional who can address more of the cognitions or beliefs that may be affecting your child and getting in the way of productive functioning.

TEACH YOUR TEENAGER TO DRIVE

Targeted Challenges: Helps teenagers who are challenged by distractibility and impulsivity learn to safely operate a vehicle.

Overview: Research studies performed by Russell Barkley, PhD, have shown that children and adults with ADHD are more likely to show poor decision making and poorer driving behaviors than other people because of their distractibility and decision-making skills. However, some teenagers do thrive behind the wheel, and the sense of independence driving fosters may engender positive changes and self-confidence across the board. Every child is different—use your wise judgment.

STRATEGY IMPLEMENTATION:

1. Try to start working on your child's driving skills before they turn eighteen, so you can oversee their driving before they become independent.

2. Oversee your child's driving practice, and motivate them to practice by offering rewards. Try to keep initial practice times short, such as thirty minutes, to reduce potential burnout for both you and your child.

3. Inform your child about how their ADHD symptoms might affect their driving to increase their awareness. For example, remind them of how inattention and distractibility can worsen driving skills and decrease safety. Work with them to identify distracting factors that can pose problems for their driving, such as driving with loud friends, driving while talking or listening to music, driving when tired, driving very long distances, or driving at night.

4. Restrict driving to the daytime and set a no-tolerance policy about drinking and texting while driving.

5. Keep in mind that, according to research conducted by Barkley, the only known tool to improve the driving of teens with ADHD is stimulant medication (when recommended by a qualified physician). If this type of medication is recommended for your child, be sure their dose is correct and that they are taking the medication at the right time before they start to drive.

6. Ask your teen to keep track of where and when they drive at first so that you can stay informed and ensure safety.

7. Remind your teen that the rules about driving are non-negotiable and must be followed for the privilege of using the car.

Helpful Modifications and Tools: Use Worksheet #4, a behavioral contract, to enforce what your child needs to do, such as driving to school with no passengers, to receive use of the car. Agree with your child about the consequences for not following the rules, such as loss of the car for a period of time, and put these consequences in writing into the contract.

If your child does not follow the rules and responsibilities of the behavioral contract, follow through with the agreed-upon consequences immediately. Resist the temptation to argue with your child. Instead, remind them that these rules were agreed upon in advance and that they must follow them in order to drive.

Visit the CHADD website (see the Resources section on page 148) to learn more about the driving program developed by Russell Barkley, PhD. Barkley has extensively studied statistics related to the dangers of teens with ADHD at the wheel. This program involves a monitored progression through three levels of driving before teens reach independence as drivers. During level one, teens drive only during the day. During level two, teens drive until 9 or 10 p.m. Driving at later hours starts at level three. Teens have to continue to check in with parents during each level, even after completing level three, and parents have to fill out questionnaires to determine if their children are ready to progress to the next level.

HELP YOUR TEENAGER PREPARE FOR INDEPENDENCE

Targeted Challenges: Helps teenagers whose executive function or practical skills for daily living may lag behind those of their peers.

Overview: Parents can provide their children with a great deal of structure that helps their daily functioning. However, as children get older, they need to prepare for independent living.

STRATEGY IMPLEMENTATION:

1. Help your teen find an organizational system that works for them, whether it's a paper planner, electronic calendar, or application available on iTunes such as iStudiez (see the Resources section on page 151).

2. Help your teen assess their skills in the area of independent living, including the following categories:

   - Food shopping and cooking

   - Doing laundry

   - Taking public transportation and/or learning to drive

   - Making and sticking to a budget and paying bills

   - Keeping to and executing daily tasks

   - Managing time

3. For each skill, assess what your child needs to do to function independently. Develop smaller steps to help them advance in the right direction. For example, show them how you do the laundry, and break it down into digestible steps (separating whites from colors, what kind of detergent to use and how much, which cycles for what fabric, etc.).

4. Start with simple steps, such as cooking easy-to-prepare meals or taking the local bus a short distance away, and then build to more complicated tasks.

5. Have your teen start keeping their own appointments. Periodically, you can check in with your child to make sure they continue to update and consult their organizational system on a daily level.

6. Reward your teen for carrying out small steps toward independence. For example, making dinner can be rewarded with use of the car or a slightly increased allowance.

7. If your teen is resistant to doing any of these tasks on their own, try not to do it for them. Though it may be tempting to clean their room or do their laundry, allow them to face the real consequences of not carrying out these tasks on their own. For example, they should be given the opportunity to realize that if they don't do their laundry, they won't have clean clothes to wear.

Helpful Modifications and Tools: If your teen is not able to organize their own work and tasks, they may need the help of an ADHD coach or cognitive behavioral therapist (see pages 100, 124, and 136 for more information on these strategies). They may also need to attend a more supportive college program after high school (if they plan to attend college) to help build structure and stay on top of the tasks at hand. Consult your teen's college counselor for more information about these programs. You can also consult *Applying to College for Students with ADD and LD* for more help.

FIND POSITIVE ROLE MODELS

Targeted Challenges: Helps teenagers who may show poor judgment or impulsiveness.

Overview: During the teenage years, your child may reject your help and suggestions. Therefore, your teen may need to connect with another trusted adult to provide feedback.

STRATEGY IMPLEMENTATION:

1. Find a teacher, coach, or school counselor your child connects with. That person can be a great way to model positive adult behaviors and speak to your child about choices made through adolescence.

2. Connect your child with a trusted family friend, clergyperson, or find a role model through an ADHD organization such as Children and Adults with Attention Deficit/Hyperactivity Disorder (CHADD), which is listed in the Resources section on page 148.

Long-Term Considerations: Over time, your child might get so much positive role modeling that it could lead them to volunteer to work with younger children with ADHD. This type of community service can be very positive for a teenager with ADHD—helping others can help build your teen's confidence.

CHAPTER 8

Adults
(AGE 20 AND OVER)

If your child has reached adulthood and is struggling to manage their ADHD symptoms, share the strategies in this chapter with them. These strategies will help your adult child fulfill their considerable potential and find their niche, while managing any problems they may continue to face with organization, time management, and other areas. Though your role as a parent may be different now that your child is an adult, your continued emotional support during this time can be incredibly helpful.

As children with ADHD mature into adulthood, they may find that some of their symptoms wane. For example, most adults with ADHD find that they have fewer symptoms related to inattention and hyperactivity. However, about 40 to 50 percent of adults still meet the diagnostic criteria for ADHD.

As teens with ADHD move into college or independent life, they may find that their symptoms interfere with success in some areas. For example, if they received a great deal of support and structure at home without having learned to implement strategies on their own, they may not be able to handle the long-term assignments of college, which professors expect students to plan and carry out by themselves. They also may not know how to organize their time so that they can socialize while getting work done, and they may not have the self-advocacy or organizational skills to find the help they need.

With the proper strategies in place, however, college and early adulthood can be times when people with ADHD begin to shine. If they are able to find the right kinds of help and advocate for themselves, and if they have developed organizational systems that keep them on track in managing their time and tasks, they can focus on areas of interest that motivate them and develop expertise in those areas. At the same time, they can move away from areas of study and work that have not held their attention in the past.

As people with ADHD age, the demands of later adult life including a job, personal relationships, and raising children can present additional challenges. These situations come with an increased need for organizational and time-management skills. The positive side of adult life is that people with ADHD can often find a niche in which they can shine. In fact, they may find that ADHD presents advantages, such as creativity and insight, which can be assets in a workplace that prizes flexibility and change over routine and predictability. Finding an area that caters to their interests and talents is empowering.

FIND THE RIGHT CAREER NICHE

Targeted Challenges: Helps adults with inattention and disorganization and improves self-confidence.

Overview: Adults with ADHD can find that the condition works to their advantage—if they are able to find a career that builds on their strengths while minimizing the need to perform in areas of disinterest or difficulty.

STRATEGY IMPLEMENTATION:

1. Consider how you can develop interests that you can use in a career.

2. Consult a career counselor who has experience working with people with ADHD to find a career that builds on your strengths.

3. Read books about ADHD, such as *Driven to Distraction* by Edward Hallowell and John Ratey. This book covers the nature of ADHD in adults, including the potential benefits it confers, as well as strategies for working around some of the obstacles it poses.

> **Helpful Modifications and Tools:** Consider using the help of an ADHD coach to handle ongoing difficulties, such as organizing and completing paperwork or managing deadlines. Because ADHD coaching takes into account the unique biological differences in the ADHD brain, it can help people with ADHD navigate their challenges in ways that work for them.

ADHD COACHING

Targeted Challenges: Helps adults with disorganization and time-management issues.

Overview: ADHD coaching for adults can help them develop strategies to use their strengths and overcome weaknesses to be more productive in work settings.

STRATEGY IMPLEMENTATION:

1. Find a reliable referral to a coach who is a psychologist or is trained through a known coaching institute.

2. Before you start, ask for a testimonial or to speak with one of the coach's former clients. In addition, spend fifteen to thirty minutes interviewing the potential coach. Ask whether the coach has worked with clients who have had similar issues to yours. The coach should be experienced at working with adults with ADHD. Many ADHD coaches also have ADHD themselves, so they understand the ways it can complicate your life. They can share strategies that have worked for them and might work for you, too.

3. Understand whether the coach works in person or by phone, and how the coach bills for their services. In general, it's advisable to pay for services on a session-by-session basis rather than as a package, in case you want to discontinue services at some point. However, many coaches may ask you to make a multi-session commitment, such as three months, to make sure you stick with the coaching process until you see some positive gains and progress.

4. Approach coaching with very specific goals, rather than with a vague sense of dissatisfaction about how your life is working for you. For example, some common goals for ADHD coaching

could include organizing your time and tasks more efficiently, keeping a cleaner house, getting along with coworkers or your spouse more productively, or finding a job that interests you.

5. Your coach may assign you homework to practice strategies and skills between your sessions.

6. As you work with your coach, experiment with new strategies and customize them so that they work for you. For example, part of the work might be finding a filing system that helps you keep your papers in order. Some people benefit from color-coding their systems, and others benefit from keeping their papers in open files so they can see them.

7. Try different approaches until you find the strategy that works for you, and tweak it to your specific needs. Keep in mind that you may encounter roadblocks or dead-ends as you are trying and implementing new strategies; work with your coach to get around these obstacles.

8. Your coach may want to involve other people in your life, such as your boss or spouse in the coaching process, if they are open to doing so. The coach can get others involved in helping you achieve your goals.

Helpful Modifications and Tools: If you continue to struggle with disorganization, consider consulting a doctor about starting medication or changing your dose, and investigate whether you also need the help of a cognitive behavioral therapist.

INVESTIGATE COGNITIVE BEHAVIORAL THERAPY

Targeted Challenges: Helps adults with problematic behaviors or beliefs and with coexisting conditions such as anxiety and depression.

Overview: In controlled research studies, cognitive behavioral therapy (CBT) in combination with medication has been shown to be more effective than medication alone. CBT can provide adults with ADHD with specific strategies to manage their disorganization, and it can help work with the flawed beliefs and negative thoughts that plague many adults with ADHD, which may cause them to feel anxious or depressed. In part, the therapy is effective because it offers practical strategies to combat negative thoughts, such as overgeneralization, or all-or-nothing thinking, which often affect many adults with ADHD. All-or-nothing thinking, for example, causes people to look at situations in very black-and-white ways and to think they are failures if they do not achieve perfection.

STRATEGY IMPLEMENTATION:

1. Ask your doctor or a trusted friend for a referral to a cognitive behavioral therapist. The therapist should have experience working with adults with ADHD and any other coexisting conditions.

2. Use the therapy to develop strategies to get organized, stay focused, and develop positive relationships with others.

> **Helpful Modifications and Tools:** If the therapy is not working as well as you think it should, involve your family or significant other. Much of the work involves working on relationships, and your partner can play a vital role in making the therapy effective.

OUTSOURCE TASKS

Targeted Challenges: Helps adults with disorganization and poor time management.

Overview: Outsourcing daily or work tasks can free an adult with ADHD from having to perform tedious activities, so that they can do more of what they enjoy, in both work and leisure.

STRATEGY IMPLEMENTATION:

1. Think about the tasks at work that you can outsource. For example, common duties that owners of small businesses outsource include payroll, administrative support, marketing, social media support, and bookkeeping.

2. Use well-established online sites that handle responsibilities in the preceding areas. In addition, you can use websites such as LinkedIn to search for potential employees and help you with hiring.

3. Hire a personal assistant on a task-by-task basis to carry out activities that you don't have the time or attention to do yourself and to create a realistic schedule for tasks that need to get done.

> **Helpful Modifications and Tools:** Consult Internet services that allow you to hire virtual personal assistants on an hourly basis. Two such sites are Zirtual and Tasks EveryDay (see the Resources section on page 148). Other services offered are bookkeeping, web design, and MBA consultation.

FIND STRATEGIES TO MANAGE TIME AND TRACK YOUR DEVICES

Targeted Challenges: Helps adults with disorganization and poor time management.

Overview: *There are many electronic devices and apps on the market that can help adults with ADHD keep track of their possessions and organize time.*

STRATEGY IMPLEMENTATION:

1. Find an organizational system that works for you. One example is Things, a task manager app. This program helps you break down large tasks into more manageable tasks when you enter what you need to do and a due date (see the Resources section on page 151). Another popular application, Wunderlist, allows you to sync your lists across multiple devices so that you can access your to-do lists quickly and easily. Even better, the app is free and works with many different operating systems.

2. Look for the right device for tracking your belongings. For example, the "Now You can Find It!" Wireless Electronic Locator by Sharper Image includes eight colored fobs that you can connect to easily lost devices, and if lost, a remote control helps find them.

3. Build in external reminders of time and set alarms on your smartphone to remind you that time is passing or that you have an upcoming appointment.

4. Get rid of keys by installing keyless locks. For example, Smart Home Home Automation Superstore (see the Resources section on page 151) has a variety of wireless products, including keyless locks, so you no longer need to use—and keep track of—your keys.

5. Designate special places for important items like your keys, wallet, and cell phone. They can be anywhere—a hook by the door, a small trinket dish in the bedroom, the corner of a bookshelf—but pick places where it would be easy to find the items. Then get in the habit of keeping your items in these special places whenever they are not in use.

Helpful Modifications and Tools: Read *ADDitude*, a magazine for people with ADHD (additudemag.com), to discover various strategies, applications, and devices to stay organized and manage your time, along with other information you might find helpful. Also, review the Resource section on page 148 to find links to other helpful tracking applications.

SEEK OUT PEOPLE TO HELP BALANCE YOU AND WORK ON INTERPERSONAL ISSUES

Targeted Challenges: Helps adults with inattention or disorganization at work or home.

Overview: Adults with ADHD may benefit from being with people who offer a balancing presence to support their strengths and offer help with challenges at home, work, or in personal relationships.

STRATEGY IMPLEMENTATION:

1. At work, identify the skills you excel at and those where you may need more help. For example, you may be adept at making presentations but struggle to keep track of the department's expenses.

2. Identify a trusted coworker or colleague who balances you by offering skills in areas where you are not as strong. Offer to perform work in your area of strength; an example would be giving presentations for that person, in exchange for the other person doing something you are not as comfortable with, such as keeping expense reports.

3. Balance your tasks with your significant other. Adults with ADHD often find that there is friction in their partnerships because they are not always adept at handling organizational tasks at home. Spouses and domestic partners can balance responsibilities by handling what each is best at. For example, you may not mind picking up the kids, while your partner or spouse might be better at doing the taxes. Don't feel that you have to split each task in half.

4. Realize how ADHD can affect your relationships. For example, one person's distraction issues may cause their partner or spouse to experience feelings of loneliness and rejection. The partner can also feel frustrated and angry in reaction to the inability of the ADHD adult to complete tasks or manage time. Marriages and relationships in which a partner has ADHD may require counseling or additional understanding.

5. Consult books such as *The ADHD Effect on Marriage: Understand and Rebuild Your Relationship in 6 Steps* by Melissa Orlov. This book helps couples identify the issues that ADHD poses in their relationship and customizes coping strategies that work for them.

Helpful Modifications and Tools: Consult with an ADHD coach to strategize how to approach your colleagues or supervisor about exchanging tasks at work. An ADHD coach or therapist can help you think about how to best communicate with your partner or spouse about common issues, like dividing domestic tasks, or other interpersonal challenges posed by ADHD.

If you are continually experiencing friction with your colleagues or spouse/partner, you may need to enter into therapy, such as CBT to help you build the skills to get along with others at work and home and to deal with some of the contentious issues that naturally arise in relationships. In addition, CBT can help you deal with feelings of inadequacy and depression, which may be affecting your behavior at work or home.

INVESTIGATE MEDICATION

Targeted Challenges: Helps adults with inattention, hyperactivity, and impulsivity.

Overview: Many adults with ADHD continue or start to take medication to manage symptoms.

STRATEGY IMPLEMENTATION:

1. Work with a practitioner trained in helping adults with ADHD. Ask for a referral from your family physician or from a trusted friend.

2. Investigate medications with the help of your doctor. The same types of medications that work for children with ADHD work for adults with ADHD. Be aware that some of these medications are tightly controlled substances and may require monthly doctor visits for you to obtain prescription refills.

3. When working with a physician, be sure to share any coexisting psychological or health conditions, as these conditions will help them prescribe medication that helps with symptoms without worsening other conditions. Many adults with ADHD have coexisting anxiety, depression, or bipolar disorder, so it is imperative to share this information with your doctor if it pertains to you. This is especially true if you're taking medication to treat coexisting conditions.

4. Determine how long you will stay on the medication, which is an individualized choice between you and your doctor. While children and college students often just take medication during the school year, as an adult, you can choose when you need to take the medication to manage your symptoms, as long as you consult with your physician.

Helpful Modifications and Tools: Be sure to follow up with your doctor after you start your medication to report any side effects, such as insomnia, agitation, nausea, and changes in blood pressure and pulse, and to assess the effectiveness of the medication.

BIBLIOTHERAPY

Targeted Challenges: Helps adults increase self-confidence, self-awareness, and knowledge base.

Overview: Reading about ADHD helps adults with ADHD stay abreast of new research, refined strategies, innovative treatment approaches, and tried-and-true advice and suggestions.

STRATEGY IMPLEMENTATION:

1. Continue to read books and magazines about ADHD to refine your understanding of ADHD and the benefits it provides, as well as new strategies that help you manage its symptoms.

2. Start with *Driven to Distraction* by Edward Hallowell and John Ratey. This book provides an overview of ADHD and includes stories of people with ADHD who have been successful. Other titles of interest include *The Disorganized Mind: Coaching Your ADHD Brain to Take Control of Your Time, Tasks, and Talents* by Nancy A. Ratey. This book, written by an ADHD coach, provides concrete strategies to help adults with ADHD manage their time and get organized at work and at home.

3. Review the Resources section on page 148 for these and additional titles about ADHD. There are also titles specifically focused on women with ADHD, including *Women with Attention Deficit Disorder: Embrace Your Differences and Transform Your Life* by Sari Solden. Many of these titles are also available as e-books and audio books.

> **Helpful Modifications and Tools:** *ADDitude* magazine offers readable articles that offer practical, concrete coping strategies, as well as information about different types of therapies for adults and children with ADHD (see the Resources section on page 148).

CONCLUSION

Now that you are ready to start implementing some of the strategies in this book, you may feel somewhat overwhelmed by all the choices. Keep in mind that helping your child is a continuing process, as your child will continue to grow and develop over the years. Their path to maturation and self-fulfillment may be filled with bumps and detours, but the same is true with any child. Nevertheless, their path may be a little more challenging. Rest assured, they will get there with your help. These strategies and tools have worked for many children with ADHD, and most are backed by research. In the process of helping your child, you may reach points that you consider failures or dead-ends. Look at these points as opportunities to reevaluate your parenting plan and work with your child's team to find new strategies that do help.

As you implement the strategies that work for your particular child, you will notice changes and improvements over time. If you haven't seen any progress yet despite making some changes, don't fret. You will, with time. Your child will develop skills to organize their belongings and time, deal with frustration, curb impulsive behaviors, develop an awareness of the way their mind works, and find areas of strength. These changes may be slow at times, but you will see them if you patiently stay the course and work alongside the team dedicated to helping your child.

In my practice, I have worked with many children who were impulsive and distractible, particularly during the middle school years. One boy I worked with was doing so poorly in middle school that his teachers had given up hope. When he was caught smoking near the school when he should have been in class, he was expelled.

The situation looked dire. However, his behaviors were a cry for help, which thankfully his parents realized. With this new awareness, his parents enrolled him in a school that fostered his interests. He worked with a learning specialist and developed strategies to organize himself and get his work done. And by working with a dedicated psychiatrist, the student not only found medication that helped to curb his ADHD symptoms, but he also developed the motivation and strategies to stop smoking.

He realized that getting expelled for smoking was the best thing that had ever happened to him, because it enabled him and his parents to discern that there was an issue with the educational program he was enrolled in due to his ADHD and to thus evaluate what type of school environment would inspire him to thrive. Along the way, he developed the ability to advocate for himself. As he headed off to college, he had a much better sense than most college students about what inspired him and what he needed to do to get his work done. Unlike most first-year college students, he was able to make a detailed plan about how he was going to complete his work each week, and he knew that he needed to study in the library where there were fewer distractions. He went on to excel in college and started a career in his area of interest.

This is only one story among many. It is natural for parents to be worried that their children, while maturing, will never reach a place of happiness and self-fulfillment. However, with parents who advocate for their children, ask for accommodations and modifications at school, and work with a team to help their children develop organizational, academic, and life skills, children will likely get to a place where they will be happy and productive and not require as much support.

If you are just starting your journey or even if you have been on the course for a while, remind yourself that the process can be a long one, but time is on your side. As children grow, their brains grow, too, and they eventually reach a point where self-reflection and judgment become more natural. Different children reach these milestones at different times, so don't despair if your child is lagging behind. In time, your child will reach these milestones.

Remember that there are many people who can help you and your child. Reaching out to others is not a sign of weakness but a sign of strength. Years ago, many parents were on this journey alone, but now there are many types of professionals trained to help children with ADHD. In addition, teachers and school personnel are more knowledgeable about ADHD than they were in the past. If your child has teachers who don't seem to understand ADHD, reach out to a school psychologist, social worker, or an outside professional who can educate your child's teachers about the needs—and strengths—of children with ADHD.

In the process of taking care of your child, be sure to take care of yourself, too. If you too have ADHD, you can benefit from many of the strategies offered in this book as well. Whether for your child or for both you and your child, professional help is available. Always remember, too, that you can also connect with other adults who are on this journey with their own children. You are not alone, and, as this book shows you, there's a world of support and opportunity just waiting to be tapped into.

RESOURCES

Books

Amen, Daniel G. *Healing ADD Revised Edition: The Breakthrough Program That Allows You to See and Heal the 7 Types of ADD.* Rev. ed. New York: Berkley, 2013.

> *The author recognized seven types of ADHD, discusses them, and helps readers come up with strategies for each type.*

Barkley, Russell A. *Taking Charge of Adult ADHD.* New York: Guilford Press, 2010.

Barkley, Russell A. *Taking Charge of ADHD: The Complete, Authoritative Guide for Parents.* 3rd ed. New York: Guilford Press, 2013.

> *Dr. Barkley is one of the most distinguished researchers in the field of ADHD, and his books provide strategies to help adults and parents identify and cope with ADHD.*

Dawson, Peg, and Richard Guare. *Smart but Scattered: The Revolutionary "Executive Skills" Approach to Helping Kids Reach Their Potential.* New York: Guilford Press, 2009.

> *This book focuses on "executive function skills," including the ability to plan, organize, and execute their work, and helps parents identify their children's strengths and challenges.*

Grossberg, Blythe. *Applying to College for Students with ADD and LD: A Guide to Keep You (and Your Parents) Sane, Satisfied, and Organized through the Application Process.* Washington, DC: Magination Press, 2010.

> *Blythe Grossberg helps high school students with ADHD and/or learning disorders and their parents navigate each step in the college admissions process and think about how to prepare for college studies and independent life.*

Grossberg, Blythe. *Making ADD Work: On-the-Job Strategies for Coping with Attention Deficit Disorder.* New York: Perigee, 2005.

This book helps adults with ADHD learn strategies to cope with symptoms of ADHD and use their strengths to achieve success in the workplace.

Hallowell, Edward M. and John J. Ratey. *Driven to Distraction: Recognizing and Coping with Attention Deficit Disorder from Childhood Through Adulthood.* Rev. ed. New York: Anchor, 2011.

Initially published in 2010, this book explains ADHD, dispels common myths, and highlights the positive qualities that ADHD confers.

Hoopmann, Kathy. *All Dogs Have ADHD.* Philadelphia: Jessica Kingsley Publishers, 2005.

Recommended for younger readers, this book includes charming color photographs that introduce people to some of the characteristics of people with ADHD by using dogs.

Kelly, Kate and Peggy Ramundo. *You Mean I'm Not Lazy, Stupid or Crazy?! A Self-Help Book for Adults with Attention Deficit Disorder.* Rev. ed. New York: Scribner, 2006.

This groundbreaking book, one of the first about adults with ADHD, provides information and strategies to help adults manage their ADHD.

Matlen, Terry. *Survival Tips for Women with ADHD: Beyond Piles, Palms, & Post-Its* Plantation, FL: Specialty Press/ADD Warehouse, 2005.

In the form of an easy-to-read manual, this book provides strategies to help women with ADHD.

Nadeau, Kathleen G., Ellen B. Littman, and Patricia O. Quinn. *Understanding Girls with ADHD: How They Feel and Why They Do What They Do.* 2nd ed. Saratoga, Springs, NY: Advantage Press, 2015.

ADHD often manifests itself differently in girls. The authors explain what the signs are, why girls are often undiagnosed, and their special needs in school, home, and their social world.

Orlov, Melissa. *The ADHD Effect on Marriage: Understand and Rebuild Your Relationship in 6 Steps.* Plantation, FL: Specialty Press/ADD Warehouse, 2010.

This book helps couples by identifying the issues that ADHD can pose in a marriage, and strategies that couples can customize to help them.

Quinn, Patricia O., and Judith M. Stern. *Putting on the Brakes; Understanding and Taking Control of Your ADD or ADHD*. 3rd ed. Washington, DC: Magination Press, 2012.

> *This book provides strategies to help children with ADHD inside and outside school.*

Ratey, Nancy A. *The Disorganized Mind: Coaching Your ADHD Brain to Take Control of Your Time, Tasks, and Talents*. New York: St. Martin's Press, 2008.

> *Nancy Ratey, an ADD coach, provides concrete ideas to help adults with ADHD get organized, manage their time, and improve their focus at home and at work.*

Solden, Sari. *Women with Attention Deficit Disorder: Embrace Your Differences and Transform Your Life*. 2nd ed. Nevada City, CA: Underwood Books, 2005.

> *This groundbreaking book revealed that many women suffer from ADHD, and provides information and strategies to help women with ADHD.*

Websites

ADDitude Magazine: www.additudemag.com. An online magazine for people with ADHD. Includes articles and other resources.

American Psychological Association: www.apa.org. Provides articles and resources for children and adults with ADHD.

Association for Behavioral and Cognitive Therapies (ABCT): www.abct .org. Maintains a list of therapists trained in CBT and provides a therapist finder tool.

Center for Disease Control and Prevention (CDC): www.cdc.gov. Link to ADHD-specific information: http://www.cdc.gov/ncbddd/kids /adhd.html.

Children and Adults with Attention-Deficit/Hyperactivity Disorder: www.chadd.org. Link to the ADHD Safe Driving Program: http://www .chadd.org/Portals/0/AM/Images/Understading/Safe_Driving _Program_12_07.pdf.

Department of Education: www.ed.gov. Link to information on Individualized Education Programs (IEPs): http://www2.ed.gov/parents/needs /speced/iepguide/index.html#process.

Feingold Diet: www.feingold.org. Provides information about the Feingold Diet.

National Resource Center on ADHD: www.help4adhd.org. The National Resource Center on ADHD (NRC) is the nation's clearinghouse for the latest evidence-based information on ADHD. The NRC is funded by the Centers for Disease Control and Prevention (CDC) and the National Center on Birth Defects and Developmental Disabilities.

Project Meditation: www.project-meditation.org. Link to information on visualization during meditation: http://www.project-meditation. org/a_mt4/meditation_visualization_techniques.html.

Wrightslaw: www.wrightslaw.com. Provides information about special education law and advocacy for children with disabilities, including 504 plans and the Individuals with Disabilities Education Act (IDEA), among other legal issues.

Software, Applications, and Other Tools

Cogmed: www.cogmed.com. Helps people with attention problems caused by issues with their working memory. App for Apple and Android.

iStudiez: www.istudentpro.com. Helps students track assignments and record grades.

"Now You Can Find It!" Wireless Electronic Locator by Sharper Image: Available from various sellers, product includes eight colored fobs that can be attached to objects for easy location when lost.

RescueTime: www.rescuetime.com. Allows people to track how they spend time on their computers and on the Internet and includes a blocking device. Available for PC, Mac, and Android.

SmartHome: www.smarthome.com. Offers keyless locks, among other projects, that can help people who often lose track of their keys.

Tasks Everyday: www.taskseveryday.com. Offers assistance from virtual assistants based in India who can be hired on an hourly basis.

Things (Task Manager): culturedcode.com/things. Personal task management application for MAC and IOS.

White Noise by TMSOFT: Available from iTunes. An ambient noise application for Mac and Android.

Zirtual: www.zirtual.com: Dedicated virtual assistants for entrepreneurs, professionals, and small teams.

REFERENCES

ADDitude. "Common Comorbid Conditions Associated with ADHD."
Accessed April 29, 2015. www.additudemag.com/adhd/article
/1476.html.

Alfers, Cory. "Famous People with ADHD." *Dr.CoryAlfers.com*.
Accessed April 29, 2015. www.drcoryalfers.com/famous-people
-with-adhd.

Archer, Dale. "ADHD: The Entrepreneur's Superpower." *Forbes*.
May 14, 2014. Accessed April 29, 2015. www.forbes.com/sites
/dalearcher/2014/05/14/adhd-the-entrepreneurs-superpower.

Barkley, Russell. *Taking Charge of Adult ADHD*. New York: Guilford
Press, 2010.

CHADD. "Driving and ADHD." Accessed May 1, 2015. www.chadd.org
/Understanding-ADHD/Parents-Caregivers-of-Children-with
-ADHD/Adolescents-and-Young-Adults/Driving-and-ADHD.aspx.

Connolly, Maureen. "ADD Women and Girls: Late Diagnosis, Little
Treatment." *ADDitude*. Accessed April 29, 2015. www.additudemag
.com/adhd/article/1626.html.

Dweck, Carol S. "The Perils and Promises of Praise." *EL: Educational
Leadership* 65, no. 2 (October 2007): 34–39. Accessed April 30, 2015.
www.ascd.org/publications/educational-leadership/oct07/vol65
/num02/the-Perils-and-Promises-of-praise.aspx.

Feingold Association of the United States. Accessed April 30, 2015. http://www.feingold.org.

Freitag, Christine Margarete and Wolfgang Retz. "Family and Twin Studies in Attention-Deficit Hyperactivity Disorder." *Key Issues in Mental Health* 176 (2010): 38–57. www.karger.com/ProdukteDB /Katalogteile/isbn3_8055/_92/_37/KIMH176_02.pdf.

Harvard Health Publications. "Diet and attention deficit hyperactivity disorder." November 19, 2014. Accessed on April 30, 2015. www. health.harvard.edu/newsletter_article/Diet-and-attention-deficit -hyperactivity-disorder.

Levine, Adam. "Maroon 5's Adam Levine: 'ADHD Isn't a Bad Thing.'" *ADDitude*. Accessed April 29. 2015. www.additudemag.com/adhd /article/10112.html.

National Institute of Mental Health. "Brain Matures a Few Years Late in ADHD, but Follows Normal Pattern." Accessed April 29, 2015. www.nimh.nih.gov/news/science-news/2007/brain-matures-a -few-years-late-in-adhd-but-follows-normal-pattern.shtml.

National Institute of Mental Health. "Preschoolers with ADHD Improve with Low Doses of Medication." Accessed April 29, 2015. www.nimh.nih.gov/news/science-news/2006/preschoolers-with -adhd-improve-with-low-doses-of-medication.shtml.

National Institute of Mental Health. "What is Attention Deficit Hyperactivity Disorder (ADHD, ADD)?" Accessed April 29, 2015. http://www.nimh.nih.gov/health/topics/attention-deficit -hyperactivity-disorder-adhd/index.shtml.

Smith, Brendan L. "ADHD among preschoolers." *American Psychology Association* 42, no. 7 (2011). http://www.apa.org /monitor/2011/07-08/adhd.aspx.

Spencer, T. J., J. Biederman, B. K. Madras, D. D. Dougherty, et al. "Further evidence of dopamine transporter dysregulation in ADHD: a controlled PET imaging study using altropane." *Biological Psychiatry* 62, no. 9 (Nov 1, 2007): 1059–61. http://www.ncbi.nlm.nih.gov/pubmed/17511972.

Wedge, Marilyn. "Why French Kids Don't Have ADHD." *Psychology Today*. March, 8 2012. Accessed April 29, 2015. https://www.psychologytoday.com/blog/suffer-the-children/201203/why-french-kids-dont-have-adhd.

ADHD CHALLENGES AND SYMPTOMS INDEX

INDEX

CPSIA information can be obtained
at www.ICGtesting.com
Printed in the USA
LVHW070733101119
636687LV00007B/3/P